蓝色创优规划教材

港口航道与海岸工程专业英语

主　编　郑艳娜　杨章峰

副主编　辛　凌　刘昌凤　崔　蕾

东南大学出版社
SOUTHEAST UNIVERSITY PRESS
·南京·

图书在版编目(CIP)数据

港口航道与海岸工程专业英语 / 郑艳娜,杨章峰主编.
—南京:东南大学出版社,2017.2(2025.1重印)
蓝色创优规划教材 / 陈昌平主编
ISBN 978-7-5641-7029-5

Ⅰ.①港… Ⅱ.①郑… ②杨… Ⅲ.①港口工程—英语—高等学校—教材 ②航道工程—英语—高等学校—教材 ③海岸工程—英语—高等学校—教材 Ⅳ.①U6②P753

中国版本图书馆CIP数据核字(2017)第013349号

港口航道与海岸工程专业英语

出版发行	东南大学出版社
出 版 人	江建中
社　　址	南京市四牌楼2号(邮编:210096)
网　　址	http://www.seupress.com
责任编辑	孙松茜(E-mail:ssq19972002@aliyun.com)
经　　销	全国各地新华书店
印　　刷	江苏凤凰数码印务有限公司
开　　本	787mm×1092mm　1/16
印　　张	10.75
字　　数	328千字
版　　次	2017年2月第1版
印　　次	2025年1月第4次印刷
书　　号	ISBN 978-7-5641-7029-5
定　　价	36.80元

(本社图书若有印装质量问题,请直接与营销部联系。电话:025-83791830)

目 录
Contents

Section I Basic Knowledge

Lesson 1 Civil Engineering ·· 1

Lesson 2 Hydraulic Engineering ·· 8

Lesson 3 Surveying and Mapping ··· 13

Lesson 4 Reinforced Concrete ··· 15

Lesson 5 Engineering Properties of Soils ··· 18

Lesson 6 Development of Engineering Geology in British Columbia ····························· 20

Section II Channel Engineering

Lesson 7 Inland Waterway ··· 25

Lesson 8 Inland Waterway Transport Development in China ······································ 29

Lesson 9 Fluvial Processes ··· 32

Lesson 10 Navigation Canals ·· 34

Lesson 11 Dam ··· 38

Lesson 12 Design of Weirs and Spillways ·· 43

Lesson 13 Sediment Transport ·· 47

Lesson 14 Waterway Training Structures ··· 50

Section III Port Engineering

Lesson 15 Waves ·· 54

Lesson 16 Water Depth in Harbor ·· 58

Lesson 17 Port Site Selection ··· 61

Lesson 18 Classification of Terminals by Function ··· 64

Lesson 19 Layout of Breakwater ·· 66

Lesson 20 Fender ·· 68

Section IV Coastal Engineering

Lesson 21　Artificial Island ·· 71
Lesson 22　FPSO ·· 75
Lesson 23　Gravity-wall Structures ·· 78
Lesson 24　Harbor Basin ·· 81
Lesson 25　Hong Kong-Zhuhai-Macau Bridge ·· 84
Lesson 26　Spar ·· 87

Section V Specification and Contract

Lesson 27　Choice of Structure ·· 90
Lesson 28　Loads ·· 96
Lesson 29　Design ·· 101
Lesson 30　The Contractor ·· 106

Translation for Reference 参考译文 ··· 112
参考文献 ·· 165
后记 ··· 166

Section Ⅰ Basic Knowledge

Lesson 1 Civil Engineering

Civil engineering is the planning, design, construction, and management of the built environment. This environment includes all structures built according to scientific principles, from irrigation and drainage systems to rocket launching facilities.

Civil engineers build roads, bridges, tunnels, dams, harbors, power plant, water and sewage systems, hospital, school, mass transit, and other public facilities essential to modern society and large population concentrations. They also build privately owned facilities such as airport, railroads, pipelines, skyscraper, and other large structures designed for industrial, commercial, or residential use. In addition, civil engineering plan, design, and built completed cities and towns, and more recently have been planning and design space platforms to house self-contained communities.

The word "civil" derives from the Latin for the citizen. In 1782, Englishman John Smeaton used the term to differentiate his nonmilitary engineering work from that of the military engineering who predominated at the time. Since then, the term "civil engineer" has often been used to refer to engineers who built public facilities, although the field is much broader.

Scope. Because it is so board, civil engineering is subdivided into a number of technical specialties. Depending on the type of project, the skills of many kinds of civil engineer specialists may be needed. When a project begins, the site is surveyed and mapped by civil engineers who locate utility placements-water, sewer, and power lines. Geotechnical specialists perform soil experiments to determine if the earth can bear the weight of the project. Environment specialists study the project's impact on the local area: the potential for air and groundwater pollution, the project's impact on local animal and plant life, and how the project can be designed to meet government requirements aimed at protecting the environment. Transportation specialists determine what kinds of facilities are needed to ease the burden on local roads and other transportation networks what will result from the completed project. Meanwhile, structural specialists use preliminary data to make detailed designs, plans, and specifications for the project. Supervising and coordinating the work of these civil engineer specialists, from beginning to end of the project, are the construction management specialists. Based on information supplied by the other specialists, construction management civil engineers estimate quantities and costs of materials and labor, schedule all work, order materials and equipment for the job, hire contractors and subcontractors, and perform other supervisory work to ensure the project is completed on time and as specified.

Throughout any given project, civil engineers make extensive use of computers. Computers are used to design the project's various elements (computer-aided design, or CAD) and to manage it. Computers are a necessary for the modern civil engineer because they permit the engineer to efficiently handle the large quantities of data needed in determining the best way to construct a project.

Structural engineering. In this specialty, civil engineers plan and design structures of all types, including bridges, dams, power plants, supports for equipment, special structures for offshore projects, the United States space program, transmission towers, giant astronomical and radio telescopes, and many other kinds of projects. Using computer, structural engineers determine the forces a structure must resist, its own weight, wind and hurricane forces, temperature changes that expand or contract construction of appropriate materials: steel, concrete, plastic, stone, asphalt, brick, aluminum, or other construction materials.

Water resources engineering. Civil engineers in this specialty deal with all aspects of the physical control of water. Their projects help prevent floods, supply water for cities and for irrigation, manage and control rivers and water runoff, and maintain beaches and other waterfront facilities. In addition, they design and maintain harbors, canals, and locks, build huge hydroelectric dams and smaller dams and water impoundments of all kinds, help design offshore structures, and determine the location of structures affecting navigation.

Geotechnical engineering. Civil engineers who specialize in this field analyze the properties of soils and rocks that support structures and affect structural behavior. They evaluate and work to minimize the potential settlement of buildings and other structures that stems from the pressure of their weight on the earth. These engineers also evaluate and determine how to strengthen the stability of slopes and fills and how to protect structures against earthquakes and the effect of groundwater.

Environment engineering. In this branch of engineering, civil engineers design, build, and supervise systems to provide safe drinking water and to prevent and control pollution of water supplies, both on the surface and underground. They also design, build, and supervise projects to control or eliminate pollution of the land and air. These engineers build water and wastewater treatment plants, and design air scrubbers and other devices to minimize or eliminate air pollution caused by industrial processes, incineration, or other smoke-producing activities. They also work to control toxic and hazardous wastes through the construction of special dump sites or the neutralizing of toxic and hazardous substances. In addition, the engineers design and manage sanitary landfills to prevent pollution of surrounding land.

Transportation engineering. Civil engineers working in this specialty build facilities to ensure safe and efficient movement of both people and goods. They specialize in designing and maintaining all types of transportation facilities, highways and streets, mass transit systems, railroads and airfields ports and harbors. Transportation engineers apply technological knowledge as well as consideration of the economic, political, and social factors in designing each project. They work closely with urban planners since the quality of the community is directly related to the quality of the transportation system.

Pipeline engineering. In this branch of civil engineering, engineers build pipelines and related facilities, which transport liquids, gases, or solids ranging from coal slurries (mixed coal and water) and semi-liquid wastes, to water, oil and various types of highly combustible and noncombustible gases. The engineers of determine pipeline design, the economic and environment impact of a project on regions it must traverse, the type of materials to be used—steel, concrete, plastic, or combinations of various materials—installation techniques, methods for testing pipeline strength, and controls for maintaining proper pressure and rate of flow of materials being transported. When hazardous materials are being carried, safety is a major consideration as well.

Construction engineering. Civil engineers in this field oversee the construction of a project from beginning to end. Sometimes called project engineers, they apply both technical and managerial skills, including knowledge of construction methods, planing, organizing, financing, and operating construction projects. They coordinate the activities of virtually everyone engaged in the work: the surveyors; workers who lay out and construct the temporary roads and ramps, excavate for the foundation, build the forms and pour the concrete; and workers who build the steel frame-work. These engineers also make regular progress reports to the owners of the structure.

Community and urban planning. Those engaged in this area of civil engineering may plan and develop communities within a city, or entire cities. Such planning involves far more than engineering considerations; environment, social, and economic factors in the use and development of land and natural resources are also key elements. These civil engineers coordinate needed, including streets and highways, public transportation systems, airports, port facilities, water-supply and wastewater-disposal systems, public buildings, parks, and recreational and other facilities to ensure social and economic as well as environment well-being.

Photogrammetry, surveying, and mapping. The civil engineers in this specialty precisely measure the earth's surface to obtain reliable information for locating and designing engineering projects. This practice often involves high-technology methods such as satellite and aerial surveying, and computer-processing of photographic imagery. Radio signals from satellites, scanned by laser and sonic beams, are converted to maps to provide very accurate measurements for boring tunnels, building highways and dams, plotting flood control and irrigation projects, locating subsurface geologic formations that may affect a construction project and a host of other building uses.

Other specialties. Two additional civil engineering specialties that are not entirely within the scope of civil engineering but are essential to the discipline are engineering management and engineering teaching.

Engineering management. Many civil engineers choose careers that eventually lead to management. Others are able to start their careers in management positions. The civil engineer-manager combines technical knowledge with an ability to organize and coordinate worker power, materials, machinery, and money. These engineers may work in government-municipal, country, state, or federal; in the US Army Corps of Engineers as military or civilian management engineers; or in semi-autonomous regional or city authorities or similar organization. They may also manage private engineering firms ranging in size from a few employees to hundreds.

Engineering teaching. The civil engineer who chooses a teaching career usually teaches-both graduate and undergraduate students in technical specialties. Many teaching civil engineers engage in basic research that eventually leads to technical innovations in construction materials and methods. Many also serve as consultants on engineering projects, or on technical boards and commissions associated with major projects.

New Words and Expressions

1. civil engineering 土木(民用)工程
2. irrigation 灌溉
3. drainage 排水
4. launch 发射
5. harbor 海港
6. power plant 发电厂
7. sewage 污水
8. mass transit 公共交通
9. public facilities 公共设施
10. population concentrations 人口集中
11. privately owned 私有
12. pipeline 管道
13. skyscraper 摩天楼
14. residential 住宅的
15. space platform 太空站
16. house 容纳
17. predominate 掌握,支配
18. map 测绘
19. utility 公共事业(水、电、气等)
20. placement 布局
21. sewer 污水管
22. groundwater 地下水
23. specifications 规格说明
24. contractor 承包商
25. subcontractor 分包商
26. computer-aided design 计算机辅助设计
27. structural engineering 结构工程
28. specialty 专业

29. offshore 近海的
30. transmission tower 输电塔
31. astronomical 天文学的
32. radio telescope 无线电望远镜
33. hurricane 飓风
34. asphalt 沥青
35. water resources engineering 水利资源工程
36. runoff 径流,排出的废物
37. waterfront (城市的)滨水地区
38. lock 水(船)闸
39. hydroelectric dam 水电堤坝
40. impoundment 蓄水,积水
41. geotechnical engineering 岩土工程
42. settlement 沉降
43. environment engineering 环境工程
44. supervise 监督,管理
45. wastewater treatment plant 污水处理厂
46. scrubber 洗涤器
47. incineration 焚化
48. toxic 有毒的
49. hazardous 危险的
50. dump 垃圾堆
51. neutralize (使)中和,(使)失效
52. sanitary landfill 垃圾填埋土(场)
53. transportation engineering 交通运输工程
54. airfield (飞)机场
55. pipeline engineering 管道工程
56. slurry 泥浆
57. combustible 易燃的
58. construction engineering 施工工程,建筑工程
59. oversee 监督,管理
60. project engineer 项目工程师
61. surveyor 测量员
62. lay out 放样,设计

63. ramp 斜坡
64. excavate 挖掘
65. steel frame-work 钢框架
66. community and urban planning 城市规划
67. natural resources 自然资源
68. water-supply 供水
69. satellite/aerial surveying 卫星/航空测量学
70. photographic imagery 摄影成像技术
71. laser ans sonic beam 激光束和声波束
72. boring tunnel 钻孔隧道,掘进隧道
73. geologic formation 地质构造
74. engineering firm 工程公司
75. technical board and commission 技术委员会

Lesson 2 Hydraulic Engineering

Hydraulic engineering is a branch of engineering related to the use and control of water. It is, concerned with the reasonable usage of natural water resource, such as ocean, river, lake and underground water, and the prevention of water disaster, with the help of hydraulic structures. Therefore, it is also concerned with the building of hydraulic structures and the management of such processes.

Hydraulic engineering includes such branches as waterway transportation, waterpower generation, improvement of soil by water, water supply and drainage and piscatorial water usage. In these branches, whether it be the water resource usage or it be the water disaster prevention, hydraulic structures need to be built. For example, in order to utilize the energy stored in the water, the water level should be raised by building dams to form the necessary water head needed to drive water power generators. Water-route signs, harbours, break-waters as well as special structures for ship manufacture and maintenance must be built for shipping enterprises. River routes also need to be dredged up to maintain proper functioning, and ship gates are needed. In water conservancy, projects for irrigation, drainage and flood prevention, various special structures need to be built: these are called hydraulic structures.

These various aspects of hydraulic engineering can be combined to form comprehensive projects. For example, a river can be used for shipping, energy, water supply, irrigation, fishery. A reservoir built in a river can alleviate flooding, regulate irrigation, be used for a power plant, and improve shipping and fishery.

Social and economical factors also play an important role in the planning of hydraulic engineering projects. The interests of various divisions may be in conflict, solving these conflicts in a comprehensive way is the vital for the planning of hydraulic engineering projects.

Waterway Transportation

In all types of the surface transport systems, water transport is almost as old as human habitation on this globe. Man initially exploited the resources use in water transport as a mean of travel from place to place. This resulted in the discoveries of new continents and new resources and a need of larger, better designed and equipped sea going vessel was felt. A waterway must be sufficiently deep to allow the passage of ships. Different ships have different requirements. Also navigation marks should be provided.

The potential for waterway transportation in our country is also great. Rivers that can be used for transportation total about 100,000 km. In addition, there are numerous bays and estuaries with deep water along the coastline. These are very suitable for constructing harbours. Therefore, water control and water conservancy play an important role in China. They are closely related to the lives and work of the Chinese people.

Seaport

A seaport one which provides sheltered berthing for ships and has facilities for embarking and disembarking of passengers, loading and unloading of varied cargo, storing and sorting of various consignments and servicing of ships. It is a transportation center. A harbour is the main component of a seaport which is partially enclosed water area where the ships can find refuge from storms and waves. Here, there are facilities for refueling, repairs and cargo handling and other services. Harbour structures play an important role in the hydraulic engineering, which are explained in succeeding sections of this book.

Water Power Generation

Water power schemes are some of the largest, most expensive, and most interesting civil engineering structure. We have only to think of the Niagara Falls power scheme, the Aswan High Dam or the Volta River or the Snowy Mountains projects to realize this. What is more, the construction of water powerplant is often associated with comprehensive utilization of rivers, resulting in significant advantages to national economy. The Aswan High Dam across the Nile in Upper Egypt, increases the cultivable area of Egypt by no less than 30 percent and control the flooding of the Nile and also provide 500 megawatts of electricity.

A typical water powerplant is composed of reservoir, a plant building usually made of reinforced concrete, a water turbine connected to an electric generator in the building, and other mechanical/electric equipment. A reservoir plays an important role in maintaining the balanced working condition for a hydro-power plant. The water stored in reservoir can guarantee the required flow rate for the water turbine not to be influenced by the natural variations in flow rate. This in turn guarantees that the customers can obtain the electric energies they require.

Irrigation

In agriculture, if the natural supply of water to the soil is insufficient, artificial water supply to the crops-irrigation is need to guarantee the normal growth of crops. In many cases the water is taken from a reservoir. Usually the water in a reservoir is first used for power generation and then used for irrigation. Thus, an irrigation system is built, which includes water source, water intake structure, channels, or pipes for water diversion and distribution, structures associated to the channel net, channels for discharging excessive water.

The problems associated with the design of irrigation system, e. g. determining the irrigation area, the amount of water and water source, methods for water intake and irrigation, distribution of the irrigation system, detailing of structures, etc., must be solved by collaboration among hydraulic engineers, agriculturalists, and economists.

Drainage

Drainage involves artificially removing the excessive water from a field and soil. The excessive water can be harmful to crops and may form swamps.

Drainage techniques including the following: (1) to reduce water intake by building dykes to hold back water, digging channels to stop water, etc., (2) to use drainage ditches to carry away surface water and ground water. In cities and industrialized regions, the drainage system is always underground.

Soil and Water Conversation

Soil erosion is the phenomenon of soil being washed away by wind and water. On one hand soil erosion removes surface fertile soil, and on the other hand, it increases the amount of sediment in rivers which can cause fill up and even desolation of the river. Furthermore, the erosion makes the ground less capable of being infiltrated by rain water, resulting in more frequent floods. In order to avoid these disasters, the infiltration capacity of the ground should be increased to reduce the amount and velocity of runoff. The soils should be made to increase its ability to withstand to withstand erosion. Such work of sustaining water and soil is the so-called soil and water conversation.

Flood Control

Dykes can be built to prevent river flooding. However, in most cases the dykes alone cannot finally solve the problem. With the sediment process the river bed will be gradually raised. Therefore, comprehensive measures must be taken in modern flood control. In addition to building dykes, there are still other two main aspects in flood control. One is to increase the discharge capacity of the river, e. g. by dredging up the river bed and the other is to intersect and store the flood water in the upper reaches, e. g, by building a dam there to regulate the runoff. It should be emphasized that soil and water conservation is the fundamental measure in flood control because the runoff can be significantly reduced.

Water Supply

Water supply should be be sufficient in quantity and good in quality. First, the amount of water should be estimated, and then the water source should be determined and its water quality analyzed. A water supply system includes three parts: water intake, water treatment, and water distribution. The water source has the most influence on the water supply system.

Surface water, e. g. river water, is often muddy and contains relatively large quantities of organic substance and bacteria and relatively small quantities of minerals. So it is mainly suitable for industrial usage. Ground water is usually suitable to be the water source for drinking water supply system.

The main methods of water treatment include clarification (sedimentation and filtration), sterilization and softening. Sometimes the process also includes deferrization, distillation and air elimination.

General Description of the Three Gorges Project

In the last hundred years there have been great developments in hydraulic engineering. Huge waterpower plant, canals several hundred kilometers long, and colossal irrigation and drainage projects have been built. The Three Gorges Project in China is the most famous.

The main structure of the Three Gorges Project consists of the water impounding dam, flooding releasing installations, power plants, and navigation facilities. The dam is a concrete gravity type with a max height of $175 \sim 185$ m and total length of $2,500 \sim 2,800$ m. The spillway section is built in the middle of the river channel. There are two power plants at the toe of the dam. The navigation facilities are arranged on the left bank.

New Words and Expressions

1. hydraulic 水力的,水压的
2. piscatorial 渔业的,渔民的
3. water-route sign 航标
4. hydraulic structure 水工结构
5. fishery 渔业,水产业,渔场,养鱼术
6. scheme 安排,配置,计划,阴谋,方案,图解
7. Niagara 尼亚加拉河(在加拿大和美国之间)
8. cultivable 可耕种的,可栽培的
9. megawatt 兆瓦特
10. reservoir 水库,蓄水池
11. sediment 沉积,沉淀,沉淀物,沉降
12. infiltration 渗透
13. dyke 堤坝
14. filtration 过滤,筛选,
15. sterilization 杀菌,绝育
16. deferrization 除锈,除铁
17. distillation 蒸馏,蒸馏法,蒸馏物,精华,精髓
18. colossal 巨大的,庞大的
19. Three Gorges Project 三峡工程
20. water impounding dam 蓄水大坝
21. flood releasing installation 泄洪大坝
22. spillway 溢洪道,泄洪道

Lesson 3 Surveying and Mapping

Without mapping, there could be no civil engineering, and every civil engineer therefore knows the elements of mappings, and how to gain the measurements needed to draw maps, which in English is called surveying. An area of land without hills or many buildings can be accurately surveyed with nothing but a good steel tape, but this is hard work when the land has more sides than four, or when its sides are longer than 1,000 meters. A small area with many hindrances to the lines of sight across can not be exactly surveyed with a tape, and an instrument that measures angles will then be needed. The instrument measuring angle in surveying land is called theodolite.

These instruments provide the information needed for drawing the map. But it is much simpler and more accurate to use a leveling instrument. The usual type, known as the dumpy level it fixed, like the theodolite, on a tripod, to bring the line of sight up to a convenient height above the ground, so that the surveyor can sight the surveying points without tiring. Many tripods are telescopic and their legs can be widely varied in length.

In all land surveying, the survey is built up from a series of connected triangles. The whole area should be covered by well-conditioned triangle as far as possible. With a theodolite, it is possible to get the lengths of the unmeasured side from the known angles of the triangle and measured side.

Three more pieces of surveying equipment should be mentioned, the plump bob, the plane table and the tacheometer.

The plumb bob is a weight on a string hung from the outside of a theodolite to make sure that it is centralized over the station. The plane table is a drawing board on a tripod, which can be set at various points in the field. The mapping is being done when the lengths and the angles are being measured. The tacheometer is often used with the plane table. It is an ordinary theodolite with two horizontal hair lines in the telescope which are at such a distance apart that they subtend at 100 meters a length of 1 meter. Buying noting the reading of the top and bottom hairs on a staff at a point whose distance is required, it is possible to work out the distance of the staff from the instrument. The person who is working at the instrument calls out the reading to his helper, who works out the distance between them, and multiplies it by 100, and thus obtains of the point and the instrument.

With the development of science and technology, more advanced surveying equipment has appeared. GPS (Global Positioning System) is one of them. It combines global positioning technology with computer, space and modern communication technologies.

New Words and Expressions

1. surveying 测量
2. steel tape 卷尺
3. hindrance 障碍
4. angle 角
5. theodolite 经纬仪
6. leveling 水准测量
7. dumpy level 定镜水准仪
8. tripod 三脚架
9. telescopic 望远镜的,套叠式的
10. a series of 一系列的
11. triangle 三角形
12. tacheometer 视距仪
13. plumb bob 铅锤
14. plane table 平板仪
15. subtend 对着,向着

Lesson 4　Reinforced Concrete

　　Plain concrete is formed from a hardened mixture of cement, water, fine aggregate, coarse aggregate (crushed stone or gravel), air, and often other admixtures. The plastic mix is placed and consolidated in the formwork, then cured to facilitate the acceleration of the chemical hydration reaction of the cement/water mix, resulting in hardened concrete. The finished product has high compressive strength, and low resistance to tension, such that its tensile strength is approximately one tenth of its compressive strength. Consequently, tensile and shear reinforcement in the tensile regions of sections has to be provided to compensate for the weak tension regions in the reinforced concrete element.

　　It is this deviation in the composition of a reinforced concrete section from the homogeneity of standard wood or steel sections that required a modified approach to the basic principles of structure design. The two components of the heterogeneous reinforced concrete section are to be so arranged and proportioned that optimal use is made of the materials involved. This is possible because concrete can easily be given any desired shape by placing and compacting the wet mixture of the constituent ingredients into suitable forms in which the plastic mass hardens. If the various ingredients are properly proportioned, the finished product becomes strong, durable, and, in combination with the reinforcing bars, adaptable for use as main members of any structural system.

　　The techniques necessary for placing concrete depend on the type of member to be cast: that is, whether it is a column, a beam, a wall, a slab, a foundation, a mass concrete dam, or an extension of previously placed and hardened concrete. For beams, columns, and walls, the forms should be well oiled after cleaning them, and the reinforcement should be cleared of rust and other harmful materials. In foundations, the earth should be compacted and thoroughly moistened to about 6 in. in depth to avoid absorption of the moisture present in the wet concrete. Concrete should always be placed in horizontal layers which are compacted by means of high frequency power-driven vibrators of either the immersion or external type, as the case requires, unless it is placed by pumping. It must be kept in mind, however, that over vibration can be harmful since it could cause segregation of the aggregate and bleeding of the concrete.

Hydration of the cement takes place in the presence of moisture at temperatures above 50°F. It is necessary to maintain such a condition in order that the chemical hydration reaction can take place. If drying is too rapid, surface cracking takes place. This would result in reduction of concrete strength due to cracking as well as the failure to attain full chemical hydration.

It is clear that a larger number of parameters have to be dealt with in proportioning a reinforced concrete element, such as geometrical width, depth, area of reinforcement, steel strain, concrete strain, steel stress, and so on. Consequently, trial and adjustment is necessary in the choice of concrete sections, with assumptions based on conditions at site, availability of the constituent materials, particular demands of the owners, architectural and headroom requirements, the applicable codes, and environment conditions. Such an array of parameters has to be considered because of the fact that reinforced concrete often a site-constructed composite, in contrast to the standard mill-fabricated beam and column sections in steel structures.

A trial section has to be chosen for each critical location in a structural system. The trial section has to be analyzed to determine if its nominal resisting strength is adequate to carry the applied factored load. Since more than one trial is often necessary to arrive at the required section, the first design input step generates into a series of trial-and-adjustment analyses.

The trial-and-adjustment procedures for the choice of a concrete section lead to the convergence of analysis and design. Hence every design is an analysis once a trial section is chosen. The availability of handbooks, charts, and personal computers and programs supports this approach as a more efficient, compact, and speedy instructional method compared with the traditional approach of treating the analysis of reinforced concrete separately from pure design.

New Words and Expressions

1. plain concrete 素混凝土
2. harden 使变硬,使硬化,使凝固
3. coarse aggregate 粗骨料,粗集料

4. gravel 卵石,砾石
5. admixture 外加剂,混合物
6. consolidate 捣实,巩固,压实,夯实
7. hydration 水化作用
8. compensate 偿还,补偿
9. reinforced concrete 钢筋混凝土
10. deviation 偏差,偏异,差异
11. composition 组成,构成;混合物
12. heterogeneous 不均匀性,非均质性,掺杂的
13. homogeneity 同种,同质,均质性
14. optimal 最佳的,最理想的
15. ingredient 配料,(混合物的)成分,组成材料
16. moisten 浸湿,弄湿,变潮湿
17. absorption 吸收,合并
18. immersion 插入,沉浸,浸没,浸入
19. segregation 离析,分离,分开,隔离
20. constituent $a.$ 组成的　$n.$ 组成,构成元素,组成物
21. nominal 名义上的
22. convergence 集中,收敛
23. handbook 手册,便览

Lesson 5 Engineering Properties of Soils

The properties of soils that determine their suitability for engineering use include internal friction, cohesion, compressibility, elasticity, permeability, and capillarity.

Internal friction is the resistance to sliding offered by the soil mass. Sand and gravel have higher internal friction than clays; in the latter an increase in moisture lowers the internal friction. The tendency of a soil to slide under the weight of a structure may be translated into shear; that is, a movement of a mass of a soil in a plane, either horizontal, vertical, or other. Such a sheering movement of a mass of a soil in a plane, either horizontal, vertical, or other. Such a shearing movement involves a danger of building failure.

Also resisting the danger of shear is the property of cohesion, which is the mutual attraction of soil particles due to molecular forces and the existence of moisture between them. Cohesive forces are markedly affected by the amount of moisture present. Cohesion values range from zero for dry sand to 100 kPa for very stiff clays.

Compressibility is an important soil characteristic because of the possibility of compacting the soil by rolling, tamping, vibration, or other means, thus increasing its density and load-bearing strength.

An elastic soil tends to resume its original condition after compaction. Elastic (expansible) soils are unsuitable as subgrades for flexible pavements since they compact and expand as a vehicle passes over them, causing failure of the pavement.

Permeability is the property of a soil that permits the flow of water through it. Freezing-thawing cycles in winter and wetting-drying cycles in summer alter the packing density of soil grains. Permeability can be reduced by compaction.

Capillarity causes water to rise through the soil above the normal horizontal plane of free water. In most soils numerous channels for capillary action exist; in clays, moisture may be raised as much as 30 feet by capillarity.

Density can be determined by weight and volume measurements or by special measuring devices. Stability of soils is measured by an instrument called a stabilometer, which specifically measures the horizontal pressure transmitted by a vertical load. Consolidation is the compaction or pressing together of soil that occurs under a specific load condition; this property is also tested.

News Words and Expressions

1. resume 再恢复
2. flexible 柔软的,有弹性的
3. thaw 融化
4. capillarity 毛细管作用
5. stabilometer 稳定仪

Lesson 6　Development of Engineering Geology in British Columbia

Introduction

Engineering geology is a subdiscipline of geology. Engineering geologists apply geological principles of rock, soil and groundwater to the appropriate location, design and construction of a wide variety of engineering structures, and to the assessment and design of mitigative measures for a wide variety of natural and man-made hazards. The types of projects with which engineering geologists are involved are quite different from those carried out by traditional geologists. It approaches used in their investigations also differ from those of traditional geologists.

Based on this thesis, the development of engineering geology in British Columbia can be divided roughly into three phases. Up to 1920, geology was not consciously considered in the engineering projects in the province. Between 1920 and 1945, when geological input was required or requested for an engineering project, it was usually supplied by traditional geologists. After 1945, trained and experienced engineering geologists began to practice in the province and began their involvement with the engineering projects of the day. By the 1960s, engineering geology was well established and a recognized subdiscipline of geology in British Columbia.

Engineering Geology in British Columbia

1920 to 1945

In 1921, Geological engineering began at the University of British Columbia, but only geology related to mining and petroleum geology, not civil engineering, was taught. Between 1920 and 1945, British Columbia was beginning to develop and a few larger engineering projects were under construction. In 1919, when the Department of Public Works wanted to improve navigation in the Fraser River delta, W. A. Johnson of the GSC carried out a geological investigation to determine by what engineering methods the navigable part of the river might be improved. This is possibly the first geological investigation for an engineering project in the province.

Victor Dolmage, a hardrock mining geologist with the GSC, was Chief of the

British Columbia division from 1922—1929, and mapped the bedrock geology of many parts of the province. In 1927, he started his involvement in engineering geology by carrying out geological mapping of the tunnel on Mission Mountain. In 1929, he began private consulting as a mining geologist and taught on a part time basis at UBC in the Geological Engineering program. One of his students was Dr. Jack Armstrong (referred to later). In 1930, Dolmage provided geological input for the Cleveland dam site on the Greater Vancouver Water and Sewage Board (Dolmage, unpublished). Although not trained as such, Victor Dolmage can be considered the first engineering geologist in British Columbia.

Other geologists who also contributed to some engineering projects during this period were D. F. (Cap) Kidd and H. C. Gunning, also both originally with the GSC. Kidd left the survey to form his own practice, while Gunning went to teach at UBC and later became department head of Geological Sciences and dean of Applied Science. The volume of their work in engineering and geology is minor compared with Dolmage.

1945 to 1960

The early Post-World War II years were a boom period in British Columbia. A host of dams, pulp and paper mills, tunnels and large plants were conceived, designed and constructed. While still consulting as a mining geologist, Dolmage was involved in many of these major projects including a number for British Columbia Electric such as the Bridge River Powerhouse, Wahleach power project, Cheakamus power project, Jordan River project and the W. A. C. Bennett dam. He also worked on most of the water tunnels in the Vancouver area for the Greater Vancouver Water and Sewage Board and assessed the geology of most proposed dam sites along the coast for Alcan, including the 14.5-kilometer Kemano tunnel.

By 1955, Dolmage was doing engineering geology work almost exclusively under the company name of Dolmage, Mason and Stewart. This included the demolition of Ripple Rock in Seymour Narrows for Canada Public Works in 1957, at the time the largest ever non-nuclear blast. A paper on that project, published in the Bulletin of the Canadian Institute of Mining and Metallurgy, won the Leonard Gold Medal. In 1950, in the first volume of *the British Columbia Professional Engineer*, Dolmage contributed a paper entitled Geological Examination of a Dam site.

In the 1930s and 1940s, Karl Terzaghi was a Professor of the Practice of Civil Engineering at Harvard. The only course he taught was Engineering Geology. In

1945, Terzaghi was brought to the west coast, initially in Washington but later in British Columbia, by H. A. Simons as a review consultant for soil mechanics in relation to pulp and paper mills at Port Alberni, Campbell River, Nanaimo, Crofton and Castlegar. He had a great influence on engineering geology in the province and upon his death in 1963, British Columbia Hydro renamed Mission dam, Terzaghi dam.

In the early 1950s, the British Columbia Department of Mines was the only provincial department to have any geologists on staff but they were all hardrock geologists working on mining-related projects. There was a need to provide advice on civil engineering and groundwater problems to other departments including Highways, Agriculture, Water Resources and Public Works. Consequently, Hugh Nasmith, a University of British Columbia graduate in Geological Engineering, with post graduate training in Engineering Geology from the University of Washington, was hired. He was the first trained engineering geologist to work in the province and for the province. Nasmith was involved in numerous projects from the early 1950s to 1958 when he left the department and joined R. C. Thurber and Associates, now Thurber Engineering Limited, where he continued that involvement.

In this same time period other geologists and engineering geologists came on the scene. In the late 1940s Jack Armstrong, trained as a hardrock geologist, began mapping the surficial geology of Vancouver and the Fraser Lowland which led to the publication of a GSC Paper entitled Environment and Engineering Applications of the Surficial Geology of the Fraser Lowland, British Columbia.

Doug Campbell, another classically trained geologist, was introduced to engineering geology by Dolmage. In the late 1950s he became involved in geological investigations for the W. A. C. Bennett dam. Jack Mollard, an engineering geologist, introduced air-photo interpretation to geology and engineering in the province in the late 1950s, while on a project for British Columbia Electric.

At UBC in 1959, an engineering geology program was initiated within the Geological Engineering Program, partially at the insistence of Henry Gunning.

1960 to present

Continued growth of the province has generated numerous, large, challenging engineering projects in recent years. There is a continued acceptance of engineering geology. The number of well trained and experienced engineering geologists, including some of the best in the world, has grown. Today engineering geology is practiced in a number of provincial government ministries, federal government agencies, railways and consuming firms. Although engineering geology has had little impact on bedrock mapping in British Columbia, it has stimulated research in surficial geology, geomorphology, geologic processes, groundwater and environment work. Today, engineering geologists are involved in a wide spectrum of projects, of which dams are a major area because engineering geologists know a dam site better!

News Words and Expressions

1. engineering geology 工程地质
2. subdiscipline 学科的分类
3. groundwater 地下水
4. appropriate 适当的
5. assessment 估计,估算
6. mitigative 使缓和,平息
7. aptitude 资质,才能
8. approach 方法,步骤
9. geological input 地质资料,地质信息
10. mine 采矿,采矿业
11. petroleum 石油
12. navigation 航海,航行
13. dean (大学)院长
14. boom 繁荣
15. powerhouse 发电站
16. water tunnel 过水涵洞,输水隧道
17. demolition 毁坏,爆破
18. metallurgy 冶金学
19. prairie 大草原,牧场
20. tutelage 教导,直到
21. provincial (地方)省的
22. air-photo 航拍照片
23. interpretation 译释,判读
24. initiate 开始,发动

25. insistence 坚持，坚决主张
26. ministry （政府的）部门
27. geomorphology 地形学
28. spectrum 系列，范围

Section II　Channel Engineering

Lesson 7　Inland Waterway

Navigation on inland waterways is the oldest mode of continental transport. Although during its long history it has passed through many stages of technological development and—in some countries—from prosperity to depression, there is no doubt that nowadays it forms an important and integral part of the transport infrastructure of many countries in the world.

In ancient civilizations, inland navigation flourished in the valleys of great rivers (the Nile, Euphrates, Ganges, etc.) and artificial waterways were known in ancient Egypt, Mesopotamia and China, where Emperor Yantei (Sui Dynasty AD 611) built the 'Great Canal'—a 2,400 km waterway (linking the river systems of the north with the southern provinces).

In Europe in AD 793, the Emperor Charles the Great had already started the building of a canal intended to link the Rhine and the Danube (Fossa Carolina), an attempt soon to be abandoned. The first clearly documented navigation lock dates from 1439 and was constructed on the Naviglio Grande in northern Italy.

Industrialization was the prime mover of modern waterways development in the 18th and 19th centuries with the network of navigable river sand canals in England at the forefront of this type of development (e.g. the Bridgewater canal built by James Brindley and the Ellesmere canal built by Thomas Telford). The Forth and Clyde Canal in Scotland completed in 1790, was the first sea-to-sea ship canal in the world.

The Anderton boat lift overcoming a head of 15m between the Trent & Mersey canal and the river Weaver in Cheshire, UK, was built in 1875 and is the first iron barge lift with a hydraulic lifting system.

The second half of the 19th and the beginning of the 20th century saw the construction of two great navigation canals of global importance. The 160 km long, 305 – 365 m wide and 19.5 m (minimum) deep Suez Canal opened in 1869, shortening the sea routes between Europe and the Far East by 16,000 km; nowadays it is used by 15,000 ships/year including 150,000 t oil tankers. The 80 km long Panama Canal, opened in 1914, links the Atlantic and the Pacific by a 13 km long and 153 m wide cut through the Continental Divide and a large artificial lake with three locks at the entrance and exit of the canal with a total lift of 26 m.

The present great European network of inland waterways is based on modernized and expanded 19th century navigation facilities. The same applies to the navigation facilities on the great American waterways, e. g. on the Mississippi and the Ohio River. Although in the 20th century inland waterways often could not compete with the railway and later motorway networks, they retained—and even increased—their role in the provision of a highly effective means of transport, particularly of bulk material.

The role of inland waterways in water resources management, in the provision of modern recreational facilities and in the enhancement of the environment further contributed to this new perception.

In spite of the rapid development of other modes of transport there are some universally valid advantages in transport by inland navigation (Čábelka and Gabriel, 1985):

(1) Low energy requirements (the specific energy consumption for navigation is about 80% of that for rail and less than 30% of the consumption for road transport);

(2) High productivity of labour per unit of transport output;

(3) Low material requirement per unit of transport volume (the corresponding values of rail and highway transport are two and four times higher respectively);

(4) Lowest interference with the environment (low noise, low exhaust fume generation);

(5) Very low land requirement (in the case of navigable rivers);

(6) Low accident incidence in comparison with other transport modes;

(7) Capability of easily transporting bulk cargo and large industrial products.

The detailed discussion of modes of transport on inland waterways and design and operation of associated hydraulic structures assumes that the reader is familiar with the concepts and equations of open-channel flow and at least some river engineering works.

New Words and Expressions

1. navigation 航运
2. waterway 航道；水路
3. continental 大陆的；大陆性的
4. infrastructure 基础设施；公共建设
5. Inland navigation 内陆航运
6. flourish 繁荣，兴旺；处于旺盛时期
7. lock 船闸
8. prime mover 原动力
9. canal 运河
10. bulk material 散装材料
11. contribute 贡献，出力
12. perception 认知；观念
13. consumption 消费；消耗
14. productivity 生产力；生产率
15. associate 副的；联合的
16. the Nile 尼罗河
17. Euphrates 幼发拉底河
18. Granges 恒河
19. Mesopotamia 美索不达米亚
20. Emperor Yantei 炀帝
21. Sui Dynasty 隋朝
22. the Emperor Charles the Great 查理大帝
23. Rhine 莱茵河
24. Danube 多瑙河
25. Naviglio Grande（意大利语）Grande 大运河
26. Bridgewater Canal 布里奇沃特运河
27. Ellesmere Canal 埃尔斯米尔运河
28. Trent & Mersey Canal 特伦特 & 墨西运河
29. Cheshire 柴郡（英格兰西北部的郡）
30. Suez Canal 苏伊士运河
31. Panama Canal 巴拿马运河

32. the Atlantic 大西洋
33. the Pacific 太平洋
34. the Continental Divide 大陆分水岭
35. Mississippi river 密西西比河
36. Ohio River 俄亥俄河
37. sea-to-sea ship canal 海边运河
38. boat lift 升船机
39. iron barge lift 铁驳升船机
40. hydraulic lifting system 液压升降系统
41. open-channel flow 明渠流
42. at the forefront of 在……的最前列
43. be based on 建立在……基础上
44. in the provision of 提供
45. in spite of 尽管；不管
46. in comparison with 同……比较起来

Lesson 8 Inland Waterway Transport Development in China

China, with an inland waterway system comprising more than 5,600 navigable rivers and a total navigable length of 119,000 km, has the most developed Inland Waterway Transport (IWT) subsector in the region. The majority of the country's total length of navigable waterways is located within the courses of the Yangtze, Pearl, Huaihe, and Heilongjiang rivers. The Yangtze (with its tributaries) alone has a navigable length of 58,000 km, or 50 percent of the national total, of which 3,000 km is suitable for navigation by vessels of 1,000 deadweight tonnage (DWT) or more. In addition to the major rivers, there is the ancient Beijing-Hangzhou Grand Canal, with a navigable length currently standing at 1,747 km, but which is expanding annually as a result of channel regulation works.

Within the waterway network there are about 2,000 inland ports, including 85 leading ports which provide 52 berths capable of accommodating vessels of up to DWT of 10,000. Seven of these ports each have an annual cargo throughput of at least 10 million tons. The network has some 900 navigational structures such as ship-locks and ship-lifts. Among these is the largest five-step ship-lock located at the Three Gorges Dam on the Yangtze River.

China is concentrating its IWT development thrust on 5 specific areas, namely, Yangtze River, Pearl River, Beijing-Hangzhou Grand Canal, Yangtze River Delta and the Pearl River Delta. In a proposed development in Hunan province, a US $100-million World Bank loan is being directed towards a US $220-million project aimed at bringing a greater hope for prosperity to a region where 6 million people live at subsistence level. A large part of these funds are for the provision of power generating dams, by-passing ship locking systems and a deeper waterway throughout the system permitting large vessels to undertake trade.

Meanwhile on the Yangtze (which moves 80 per cent of the country's IWT traffic) the huge commercial and infrastructure growth taking place around Shanghai—and the vast Three Gorges project (essentially to improve electric power) well upstream will completely change the scale of permissible vessel movement—above and below the dam-and opportunities for the movement of freight and people. The project includes the construction of the world's largest ship lock. The shiplock has two lines and five steps each line. The chamber dimensions of each step are 280 m long, 34 m wide and 5 m deep for passage of pushing convoy with carrying capacity of 10,000 tons. Total length of the lock is 1,607 m. Overall difference of upper and lower water levels is 113 m with the highest upper water level of 175 m. Total investment of the shiplock is US $747 million. After years of construction, the shiplock was opened for navigation on 16 June 2003.

New Words and Expressions

1. delta (河流的)三角洲
2. navigable 可通航的,可航行的
3. Inland Waterway Transport 内陆航道运输
4. subsector 界别分组
5. majority of 大多数,大部分
6. vessel 船,舰
7. deadweight tonnage 载重吨位
8. channel regulation 河道整治
9. port 港口,口岸
10. berth 泊位
11. cargo 货物船货
12. throughput 吞吐量
13. ship-lock 船闸
14. ship-lifts 升船机
15. concentrate 集中,浓缩
16. prosperity 繁荣
17. thrust *n.* 推力 *vt.* 推动,插入
18. prosperity 繁荣,成功
19. subsistence 生活,生存,存在
20. aim at 针对,瞄准,目的在于
21. freight 货运,运费,船货
22. chamber 房间,闸室

23. convoy 护航队,船队
24. carrying capacity 允许载重量
25. overall 全部地,总的说来
26. Three Gorges Dam 三峡大坝
27. thrust on 强力推进

Lesson 9 Fluvial Processes

Fluvial processes include the motion of sediment and erosion or deposition on the river bed.

Erosion by moving water can happen in two ways. Firstly, the movement of water across the bed exerts a shear stress directly onto the bed. If the cohesive strength of the substrate is lower than the shear exerted, or the bed is composed of loose sediment which can be mobilized by such stresses, then the bed will be lowered purely by clearwater flow. However, if the river carries significant quantities of sediment, this material can act as tools to enhance wear of the bed (abrasion). At the same time the fragments themselves are ground down, becoming smaller and more rounded (attrition).

Sediment in rivers is transported as either bedload (the coarser fragments which move close to the bed) or suspended load (finer fragments carried in the water). There is also a component carried as dissolved material.

For each grain size there is a specific velocity at which the grains start to move, called entrainment velocity. However the grains will continue to be transported even if the velocity falls below the entrainment velocity due to the reduced (or removed) friction between the grains and the river bed. Eventually the velocity will fall low enough for the grains to be deposited. This is shown by the Hjulström curve (as shown in Fig. 9 – 1).

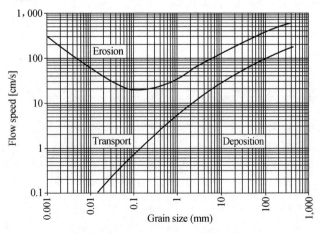

Figure 9 – 1 Hjulström curve

A river is continually picking up and dropping solid particles of rock and soil from its bed throughout its length. Where the river flow is fast, more particles are picked up than dropped. Where the river flow is slow, more particles are dropped than picked up. Areas where more particles are dropped are called alluvial or flood plains and the dropped particles are called alluvium.

The amount of matter carried by a large river is enormous. The names of many rivers derive from the color that the transported matter gives the water. For example, the Huanghe in China is literally translated "Yellow River", and the Mississippi River in the United States is also called "the Big Muddy". It has been estimated that the Mississippi River annually carries 406 million tons of sediment to the sea, the Yellow River 796 million tons, and the Po River in Italy 67 million tons.

New Words and Expressions

1. sediment 沉积,沉淀物,泥沙
2. erosion 侵蚀,腐蚀
3. deposition 沉积物
4. cohesive 凝聚的,有结合力的
5. be composed of 由……组成
6. mobilize vt. 动员,调动　vi. 组织,动员起来
7. clearwater 清水
8. abrasion 磨损,磨耗,擦伤
9. fragment 碎片,颗粒
10. be ground down 被碾碎
11. attrition 摩擦,磨损,消耗
12. bedload 推移质
13. suspended load 悬移质
14. grain 颗粒
15. dissolved 溶解的,溶化的
16. friction 摩擦力
17. alluvial 冲积的
18. alluvium [地质] 冲积层,冲积土
19. enormous 庞大的,巨大的
20. the Po River 波河
21. the Big Muddy 大泥河
22. cohesive strength 黏结强度

Lesson 10 Navigation Canals

Navigation canals can be used to bypass a river section that is difficult to navigate and can be used in conjunction with a single barrage or several barrages spaced wider apart than in the case of river canalization. Furthermore, they are an essential part of inland navigation where they connect two watersheds. They require suitably shaped intakes, often a separate flow regulation structure, and navigation locks.

The position and layout of canals can—within the traffic and geological constraints—be adapted to general transport, land-use and industrial demands. The canal is usually appreciably shorter than a canalized river which, together with low (or zero) flow velocities, aids navigation in both directions. Their main disadvantage is use of land, and disruption of communications; thus when planning a canal, maximum use should be made of existing rivers, as far as their canalization is feasible.

Navigation canals can have a fall in one direction only or in both directions with a top water reservoir. They may connect two river systems or branch off a navigable waterway to give access to an industrial centre. The crossing of a canal with a navigable river, the branching of a canal from the river or the branching of canals may create special traffic and construction problems.

Sections of canals which are either temporarily or permanently above the surrounding groundwater table need (apart from erosion protection) some means of protection against loss of water by seepage; proper underdrainage and protection of the impermeable or seepage-resistant layer (e. g. clay, concrete, plastics, etc.) against back pressure in the event of an increase of the groundwater level are essential. Bank protection on canalized rivers and canals is of the same type and variety as on trained rivers.

Adequate canal depth and width are required, just as on regulated rivers and, because of the drift of tows passing through bends, a greater width is required there. The minimum width, B, of a waterway in a straight section with simultaneous navigation in both directions is $B=3b$ or $B=2b+\Delta b$, where b is the width of a barge (or a group of barges) and Δb is the side clearance, with $\Delta b \geqslant 5$ m. If navigation is in one direction only, $B=(1.5-2)b$.

The minimum radius, r, of a curved waterway is given by the length, L, of a typical barge multiplied by a constant which is about 3 for pushboats and 4.5 for towed barges. The width of the waterway in a bend with a two-way traffic has to be increased to $B_0 = B + \Delta B$ [Fig. 10-1(a)], where

$$\Delta B = \frac{L^2}{2r+B} \simeq \frac{L^2}{2r} \tag{10.1}$$

The drift (deflection) angle, α, is the inclination of the tow to the tangent of the radius of curvature passing through the centre of the tow [Fig. 10-1(b)]. The drift depends on the radius of the bend, the speed, power, and design of the tow (tug), loading of the tow, wind forces, and the flow pattern. The drift angle is larger for tows travelling in the downstream than the upstream direction.

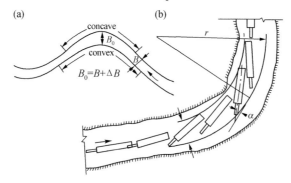

10-1 Bends and tow drift on a waterway (Novak, 1994)

The US Army Corps of Engineers (1980) extrapolated German drift angle data from the Rhine up to a tow length of 180 m and obtained, for the downstream direction, values of $2° < \alpha < 15°$ for radio of curves of 400 m $< r <$ 2,500 m (the larger the radius the smaller the value of). For the upstream direction the values of α are halved.

According to the US Army Corps of Engineers, the following equations apply for the channel width B_0 in bends:

for one-way traffic,

$$B_{01} = L_1 \sin\alpha_d + b_1 + 2c \tag{10.2}$$

and for two-way traffic,

$$B_{02} = L_1 \sin\alpha_d + b_1 + L_2 \sin\alpha_u + b_2 + 2c + c' \tag{10.3}$$

where L is the length of the tow, is the maximum drift angle, b is the width of the tow, c is the clearance between the tow and channel bank and c' is the clearance between the passing tows; suffix 'd' refers to a downbound and 'u' to an upbound tow. The result of computations using equation (10.3) can be checked against equation (10.1).

New Words and Expressions

1. bypass 绕开,设旁路,迂回
2. barrage 拦河坝
3. flow regulation 流量调节
4. watershed (美)流域,分水岭
5. layout 布局,设计
6. adapt vt. 使适应,改编 vi. 适应
7. appreciably 明显地,相当地
8. disruption of communications 断流
9. feasible 可行的,可能的
10. fall 水位落差
11. reservoir 水库
12. branch off 分叉,支流
13. canalization 运河网,开运河
14. seepage [流]渗流,渗漏
15. underdrainage 地下排水,暗渠排水
16. resistant 抵抗的,反抗的,顽固的
17. adequate 充足的,适当的
18. drift 漂流
19. tows 拖带船
20. simultaneous 同时的,联立的,同时发生的
21. clearance 空隙
22. pushboats 顶推船队
23. towed barges 拖带船队
24. the drift angle 转向角
25. inclination 倾向,斜坡,倾斜度
26. tangent [数] 切线
27. curvature 弯曲,[数] 曲率
28. loading 装载,装货,装载的货
29. extrapolate vt. 外推,推断 vi. 外推;进行推断

30. in conjunction with 连同,与……协力
31. in the case of 至于,在……的情况下
32. as far as 至于,就……而言
33. in the event of 如果……发生
34. refer to 参考,适用于,指的是
35. check against 核对,检查

Lesson 11 Dam

The first dam for which there are reliable records was built on the Nile River sometime before 4,000 B. C. it is used to divert the Nile and provide a site for the ancient city of Memphis. The oldest dam still in use is the Almanza Dam in Spain, which was constructed in the sixteenth century. With the passage of time, materials and methods of construction have improved, making possible the erection of such large dams as the Nurek Dam which is being constructed in the Former Soviet Union on the Vaksh River near the border of Afghanistan. This dam will be 1,017 ft (333 m) high, of earth and rock fill. The failure of a dam may cause serious loss of life and property; consequently, the design and maintenance of dams are commonly under government surveillance. In the United States over 30,000 dams are under the control of state authorities. The 1972 Federal Dam Safety Act (PL 92 – 267) requires periodic inspections of dams by qualified experts. The failure of the Teton Dam in Idaho in June 1976 added to the concern for dam safety in the United States.

1. Types of Dams

Dams are classified on the basis of the type and materials of construction, as gravity, arch, buttress, and earth. The first three types are usually constructed of concrete. A gravity dam depends on its own weight for stability and is usually straight in plan although sometimes slightly curved. Arch dams transmit most of the horizontal thrust of the water behind them to the abutments by arch action and have thinner cross section than comparable gravity dams. Arch dams can be used only in narrow canyons where the walls are capable of withstanding the thrust produced by the arch action. The simplest of the many types of the buttress dams is the slab type, which consists of sloping flat slabs supported at intervals by buttress. Earth dams are embankments of rock or earth with provision for controlling seepage by means of an impermeable core or upstream blanket. More than one type of dam may be included in a single structure. Curved dams may combine both gravity and arch action to achieve stability. Long dams often have a concrete river section containing spillway and sluice gates and earth or rock-fill wing dams for the remainder of their length.

The selection of the best type of dam for a given site is a problem in both engineering feasibility and cost. Feasibility is governed by topography, geology and climate. For example, because concrete spalls when subjected to alternate freezing and thawing, arch and buttress dams with thin concrete sections are sometimes avoided in areas subject to extreme cold. The relative cost of the various types of dams depends mainly on the availability of construction materials near the site and the accessibility of transportation facilities. Dams are sometimes built in stages with the second or later stages constructed a decade or longer after the first stage.

The height of a dam is defined as the difference in elevation between the roadway, or spillway crest, and the lowest part of the excavated foundation. However, figures quoted for heights of dams are often determined in other ways. Frequently the height is taken as the net height above the old river bed.

2. Forces on Dams

A dam must be relatively impervious to water and capable of resisting the forces acting on it. The most important of these forces are gravity (weight of dam), hydrostatic pressure, uplift, ice pressure, and earthquake forces. These forces are transmitted to the foundation and abutments of the dam, which react against the dam with an equal and opposite forces, the foundation reaction. The effect of hydrostatic pressure caused by sediment deposits in the reservoir and of dynamic forces caused by water flowing over the dam may require consideration in special cases.

The weight of a dam is the product of its volume and the specific weight of the material. The line of action of this force passes through the center of mass of the cross section. Hydrostatic forces may act on both the upstream and downstream faces of the dam. The horizontal component of the hydrostatic force H_h is the force on a vertical projection of the face of the dam, and for unit width of dam it is

$$H_h = rh^2/2 \qquad (11.1)$$

where: r is the specific weight of water; h is the depth of water. The line of action of this force is $h/3$ above the base of the dam. The vertical component of the hydrostatic force is equal to the weight of water vertically above the face of the dam and passes through the center of gravity of this volume of water.

Water under pressure inevitably finds its way between the dam and its foundation and creates uplift pressures. The magnitude of the uplift force depends on the character of the foundation and the construction methods. It is often assumed that the uplift pressure varies linearly from full hydrostatic pressure at the upstream face (heel) to full tail-water pressure at the downstream face (toe). For this assumption the uplift force U is

$$U = r(h_1 + h_2)t/2 \qquad (11.2)$$

Where: t is the base thickness of the dam; h_1 and h_2 are the water depths at the heel and toe of the dam, respectively. The uplift force will act through the center of area of the pressure trapezoid (Fig. 11-1).

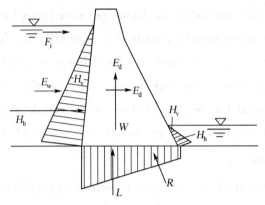

Figure 11-1 free-body diagram of the cross section of a gravity dam

Actual measurements on dams (Fig. 11-2) indicate that the uplift force is much less than that given by eq. 11.2. Various assumptions have been made regarding the distribution of uplift pressures. The U. S. Bureau of Reclamation sometimes assumes that the uplift pressure on gravity dams varies linearly from two-thirds of full uplift at the heel to zero at the toe. Drains are usually provided near the heel of the dam to permit the escape of seepage water and relieve uplift.

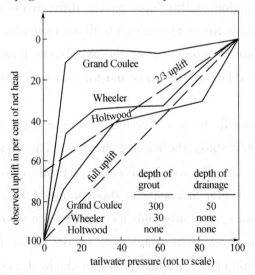

Figure 11-2 maximum observed uplift pressure under some existing gravity dams

(Data from the ASCE Committee on Uplift in Masonry Dams)

New Words and Expressions

1. reliable 可靠的
2. erection 建筑,安装
3. border 边沿,边界,田埂
4. consequently 从而,因此
5. surveilance 监视
6. periodic 周期的,定时的
7. inspection 检查,调查
8. qualified 有资格的,合格的,胜任的
9. thrust 推力
10. abutment 座,坝座
11. comparable 比较的,类似的
12. canyon 峡谷
13. slab (平)板,(厚)片
14. flat 平坦的
15. embankment 土堤,填土堤,堤防
16. seepage 渗透(漏),渗出
17. impermeable 不渗透的,不透水的
18. core 心墙,坝心
19. blanket 铺盖,覆盖层
20. remainder 剩余,余项
21. topography 地形,地势
22. geology 地质,地质学
23. spall 碎裂,剥落
24. thaw 融化,解冻
25. accessibility 接近性,可达性
26. excavate 开凿,挖掘
27. quote 引用,引证
28. impervious 透不过的
29. hydrostatic 静水(力)的,流体静力学
30. uplift 扬压力,上托力
31. inevitably 不可避免地

32. heel 坝踵，上游坡脚
33. tailwater 尾水，尾水位
34. toe 坝趾，坝脚
35. trapezoid 不规则四边形的，梯形的
36. assumption 假设
37. relieve 减轻，解脱（开）
38. the passage of time 时间的推移
39. cross section 横截面，剖面
40. curved dam 弧形坝
41. sluice gate 泄水闸门
42. rock-fill wing dams 堆石翼坝
43. spillway crest 溢洪道顶部，溢流堰顶
44. horizontal component 水平分力
45. vertical projection 垂直投影
46. seepage water 渗水
47. the Almanza Dam in Spain 西班牙的阿尔曼扎坝
48. Memphis 孟菲斯城（古埃及）
49. the Vaksh River 瓦赫什河
50. Afghanistan 阿富汗
51. the 1972 Federal Dam Safety Act 1972年（美国）联邦大坝安全法
52. the Teton Dam in Idaho 安达荷州的泰托坝
53. the U.S. Bureau of Reclamation 美国垦务局

Lesson 12 Design of Weirs and Spillways

1. Definitions: Dams and Weirs

Dams and weirs are hydraulic structures built across a stream to facilitate the storage of water.

A **dam** is defined as a large structure built across a valley to store water in the upstream reservoir. All flows up to the probable maximum flood must be confined to the designed spillway. The upstream water level should not overtop the dam wall. Dam overtopping may indeed lead to dam erosion and possibly destruction.

A conventional **weir** is a structure designed to rise the upstream water level: e. g. for feeding a diversion channel. Small flow rates are confined to a spillway channel. Larger flows are allowed to pass over the top of the full length of the weir. At the downstream end of the weir, the kinetic energy of the flow is dissipated in a dissipator structure [Figs 12 - 1(a) and 12 - 2(a)].

Another type of weirs is the **minimum energy loss weir** (**MEL**) [Figs 12 - 1(b) and 12 - 2(b)]. MEL weirs are designed to minimize the total head loss of the overflow and hence to induce (ideally) zero afflux. MEL weirs are used in flat areas and near estuaries.

Practically, the differences between a small dam and a conventional weir are small, and the terms 'weir' or 'small dam' are often interchanged.

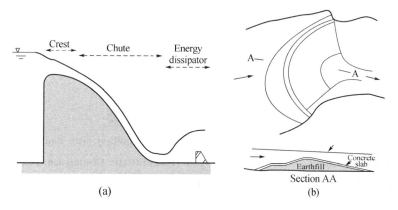

Figure 12 - 1 sketch of weirs: (a) conventional weir and (b) MEL weir

(a)   (b)

Figure 12 - 2 examples of spillway operation: (a) diversion weir at Dalby QLD, Australia on 8 November 1997. Ogee crest followed by smooth chute and energy dissipator (note fishway next to right bank). (b) overflow above an MEL weir: Chinchilla weir at low overflow on 8 November 1997. Design flow conditions: 850 m^3/s, weir height: 14 m and reservoir capacity: 9.78×10^6 m^3.

2. Overflow spillway

During large rainfall events, a large amount of water flows into the reservoir, and the reservoir level may rise above the dam crest. A spillway is a structure designed to 'spill' flood waters under controlled (i.e. *safe*) conditions. Flood waters can be discharged beneath the dam (e.g. culvert and bottom outlet), through the dam (e.g. rockfill dam) or above the dam (i.e. overflow spillway).

Most small dams are equipped with an overflow structure (called spillway) (e.g. Fig. 12 - 3) An overflow spillway includes typically three sections: a crest, a chute and an energy dissipator at the downstream end. The crest is designed to maximize the discharge capacity of the spillway. The chute is designed to pass (i.e. to carry) the flood waters above (or away from) the dam, and the energy dissipator is designed to dissipate (i.e. 'break down') the kinetic energy of the flow at the downstream end of the chute [Figs 12 - 1(a) and 12 - 2].

Figure 12 - 3 examples of spillway design: Overflow spillway with downstream flip bucket (Reece dam TAS, 1986) (courtesy of Hydro-Electric Commission Tasmania). Design spillway capacity: 4,740 m^3/s, overflow event: 365 m^3/s.

A related type of spillway is the drop structure. As its hydraulic characteristics differ significantly from that of standard overflow weirs, it will be presented in another chapter.

3. Discussion

Although a spillway is designed for specific conditions (i. e. design conditions: Q_{des} and H_{des}), it must operate safely and efficiently for a range of flow conditions.

Design engineers typically select the optimum spillway shape for the design flow conditions. They must then verify the safe operation of the spillway for a range of operating flow conditions (e. g. from 0.1 Q_{des} to Q_{des}) and for the emergency situations (i. e. $Q > Q_{des}$).

In the following sections, we present first the crest calculations, then the chute calculations followed by the energy dissipator calculations. Later the complete design procedure is described.

New Words and Expressions

1. definition 定义
2. weir 堰,坝
3. spillway 溢洪道,泄洪道
4. hydraulic structure [水利]水工建筑物
5. facilitate 促进,帮助
6. flood 洪水,洪峰流量
7. overtop 超出,凌驾
8. flow rate [水文]流量
9. destruction 破坏,毁灭,溃坝
10. conventional 符合习俗的,传统的,常规的
11. kinetic [力]运动的,活跃的
12. diversion channel 分水渠,泄水渠
13. dissipate 使……消散
14. the minium energy loss weir 最小能量损失堰
15. estuary 河口,江口
16. practically 实际地,几乎,事实上
17. crest 顶,堰顶
18. beneath 在……之下

19. culvert 涵洞
20. chute 泄水槽
21. energy dissipator 消能池
22. significantly 显著地,相当数量地
23. specific 特殊的,特定的
24. optimum 最适宜的,最优的
25. verify 核实,查证
26. emergency 紧急的,备用的
27. be confined to 限制,禁闭
28. lead to 导致,通向
29. hence 因此,今后
30. be equipped with 配备有……,装有……

Lesson 13   Sediment Transport

Sediment is transported from one place to another by flowing water. Depending on the size and degree of cohesion of the sediment grains and intensity of the flow, the amount transported may be proportional to the velocity of the flow or proportional to the velocity squared, cubed, and so on. Thus, a doubling of flow velocity may increase sediment transport as much as eightfold. In some cases, more sediment is transported in one storm event than in all the rest of the year.

The proportionality effect as described can also cause substantial sediment deposition. If a waterway's cross section is suddenly increased by increased depth or width, such as when the stage goes above bankfull, the flow velocity drops and the capacity to transport sediment falls even faster, so sediment will tend to deposit. This effect is a common cause of shoaling in navigation channels and ports, and is sometimes used to force sediment deposition in a particular location, such as a sediment trap.

Vessel traffic can suspend sediment from the bed and banks of a waterway through:

(1) Flow under and around the vessel as water moves from the bow of the vessel to the stern;

(2) Pressure fluctuations beneath the vessel;

(3) Propeller wash striking the bed; and

(4) Bow and stern waves agitating the bed and breaking against the bank.

Fig. 13-1 illustrates the surface sediment plume that can form owing to vessel passage.

Figure 13-1   surface sediment plume from vessel passage

Source: USACE Engineer Research and Development Center, Coastal and Hydraulics Laboratory

Sediment suspended by vessel traffic can either quickly settle out (if the sediment consists of sand-sized material) or remain in suspension (if the sediment consists of very fine silts or clay-sized material). A fine sediment suspension has greater density than the surrounding water, so it can flow as a density current away from the point of suspension. The latter process can move sediment from the waterway centerline into relatively quiet berthing areas, where it settles out. This phenomenon has been documented in several locations (e.g., Kelderman et al., 1998).

Eddies, which are circular flow patterns formed by flow past an obstruction or in front of an opening such as a port basin, have a complex, three dimensional circular structure with flow inward near the bottom and outward near the surface, with a quieter zone in the middle. Sediment passing near an eddy is drawn into the eddy and pushed toward the center, where it tends to deposit, much like loose tea leaves in a stirred cup. This phenomenon is a common cause of sedimentation in slips, side channels, and berthing areas.

Natural streams can be characterized by their tendency to meander and migrate, irregularities and changes in geometry, varying stages and discharges, and variations in the composition of beds and banks. Many of the problems encountered in the development and improvement of natural streams are concerned with channel alignment and the movement of sediment into and within the stream. Scouring of the bed and banks and deposition in critical areas can affect channel depth, width, and alignment, and the operation and use of facilities and structures for navigation such as locks, harbors, docking areas, and other facilities such as hydropower plants, sewage systems, and water intakes. Sediment movement can also affect the capacity of the channel to pass flood flows.

New Words and Expressions

1. cohesion 凝聚,结合,[力]内聚力
2. intensity 强度,强烈
3. proportional 比例的,成比例的
4. squared 平方的
5. eightfold 八倍的
6. proportionality 相称,均衡,比例性
7. bankfull 满水时期

8. shoaling [海洋]浅水作用,浅滩

9. stage 水位

10. sediment trap 沉积阱

11. suspend 延缓,推迟,使暂停,使悬浮

12. bow wave [航海学]船首波,船首两侧的浪花

13. stern wave 尾波

14. fluctuations [物]波动

15. propeller wash 螺旋桨尾流

16. agitate 摇动,骚动

17. density current [水利]异重流

18. relatively 相当地,相对地,比较地

19. phenomenon 现象

20. obstruction 障碍,阻碍

21. silt 淤泥,泥沙

22. eddy 涡流,漩涡

23. stirred cup 搅拌杯

24. berthing area 船只停泊区

25. meander 蜿蜒曲折

26. migrate 移动,随季节而移居,移往

27. irregularity 不规则,无规律

28. beds and banks 河床和河岸

29. encountered 遇到,曾遭遇

30. scouring 洗擦,冲刷

31. harbor 海港

32. docking area 泊船区

33. sewage system 污水下水道系统

34. channel alignment 航道线位

35. be proportional to 与……成比例

36. settle out 沉积,沉淀下来

37. consist of 由……组成,由……构成

38. be concerned with 参与,相干,涉及

39. tend to 有……的倾向

Lesson 14   Waterway Training Structures

1. General

For navigation channel works, it is obvious that there is a wide range of techniques and options available to the designer. It should be realized that the development and control of the river channel depends on the final desired objective of the particular project. Therefore, among the many and varied sizes and shapes of dikes and revetments to choose from, selection of the most effective method for a particular river situation is highly dependent on the education, knowledge, and experience of the designer. All alternatives are not necessarily applicable in all situations, and they need to be adapted to site conditions and the size of the stream being investigated. Some of the techniques are more suitable in large inland waterways, such as the Mississippi River system, whereas these same techniques may or may not be suitable for the smaller inland waterways, such as the Red River in Louisiana.

There are two types of waterway training structures: redirective and resistive. A redirective structure, as the name implies, uses the river's energy and manages that energy in a way that benefits the system, such as to enhance the navigation channel. A resistive structure acts to maintain the status quo of the system, such as to reduce bank erosion.

2. Redirecitive Structures

Redirective structures are usually a series of dikes placed along the inside of a river bend where sediment usually deposits. Dikes function continually at lower river stages; however, the effects of dikes will decrease or "wash out" when overtopped at higher river stages. The major functions of dikes are to (1) concentrate the river's energy into a single channel to control the location and increase the depth of the navigation channel, and (2) affect the erosional and depositional characteristics of the river to reshape the dimensions of the navigation channel. Dikes have been known by a variety of names throughout the years, such as groins (or groynes), transverse dikes, cross dikes, spur dikes, cross dams, wing dams, and spurs. The most common dikes in use today are shown in Fig. 14-1.

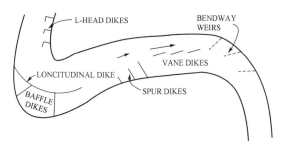

Figure 14-1　Types of dike structures (Note: River flow in the down stream direction is indicated by an arrow on this and several following figures) Source: USACE (1997)

Certain types of control works are essential in the very early phases of development of a navigation channel, whereas others are used primarily in the final refinement phases of the project. For example, the use of under water sills was never contemplated in the early design of the Missouri River navigation channel. The use of such sills was added to the project to provide additional confinement of the channel to realize the final objective, while not adversely restricting channel conveyance for high flows.

In the initial designs of early U.S. inland navigation channels, the so called environmental type of modifications presented in Chapter 10, were not originally considered. The vast majority of the inland navigation systems in the United States were designed and constructed long before environmental considerations were considered as valuable attributes to channel training works. In fact, environmental modifications were implemented over time as design priorities changed. Therefore, modifications to some types of training works, such as dikes, provided environmental enhancement while maintaining their original purpose of contracting the navigation channel and reducing maintenance dredging.

3. Resistive structures

Resistive structures are primarily used to prevent bank erosion and channel migration on the outside of a river bend, and to establish or maintain a desired channel alignment. Revetments are usually made of rock but, in the case of the lower Mississippi River, ACMs have been used effectively. Fig. 14-2 shows a typical rock revetment.

Figure 14-2 stone revetment protecting a Mississippi River bankline
Source：USACE Vicksburg District

New Words and Expressions

1. obvious 明显的,显著的
2. realize 实现,认识到
3. particular 特别的,独有的
4. dike 堤,堤坝
5. revetment 护岸
6. alternative 供替代的选择
7. applicable 可适用的,可应用的
8. site conditions 现场环境
9. investigate 调查,研究
10. whereas 然而,鉴于,反之
11. The Red River 红河
12. redirective 堤防
13. resistive 护岸
14. benefit 有益于,对……有益
15. status quo 现状
16. river stage 河流水位
17. concentrate 集中,浓缩
18. reshape 改造,再成形
19. groin 丁坝
20. groyne 防波堤
21. transverse dike 横堤
22. wing dams 翼坝

23. spur dike 丁堤
24. primarily 首先，主要地，根本上
25. refinement phases 完善阶段
26. confinement 限制
27. sill 窗台，基石
28. adversely 不利地，逆地，反对地
29. restricting 限制
30. conveyance 运输
31. environmental 环境的，有关环境的
32. implement 实施，执行
33. priority 优先，优先权
34. maintain 维持，继续
35. dredge （用挖泥船等）疏浚
36. maintenance 维护，维修
37. migration 迁移

Section Ⅲ Port Engineering

Lesson 15 Waves

Wave Action in Ports

Wave action is important for any harbor during its construction and for its performance after construction has been completed. Wave force is important for the design of structures, for maneuvering of vessels, and for mooring and berthing. Wave conditions can have a significant bearing on navigation channel design. Wave affects design channel depths and widths.

Port on open-sea coast must be protected against wave action. Of course, design considerations are not the same for short and long-period wave actions because the behaviors of the two types of waves are very different. For short-period wave action, the question of permissible wave action in ports can be concluded. Acceptable wave heights increase as the size of the ship increases. The critical limit is lowest for beam seas and highest for head sea. Ships less than 30,000 DWT should not be exposed to waves bigger than 1 meter in port. Vessels larger than 30,000 DWT should not experience larger movements in roll and yaw than 0.5 meter. For long-period waves' action in harbors, various researches have demonstrated that long-period are coupled to short wave systems. It is impossible to prevent the penetration of long-period waves ($\geq$30 seconds) into a harbor, unless the entrance is closed. Problems of long wave activity are usually much tougher to handle than short wave problems. Adverse effects by long-period waves in port basins may be eliminated to considerable extent by avoiding natural conditions and basic geometry which encourage resonance phenomena.

Regardless of whether short-period or long-period wave is the subject, the problem of resonance is very important. Wind waves or swells of 10 - 20 seconds may cause a resonances effect in shorter harbor basins, e.g, when the period, T, of a free oscillation having its mode at the entrance and its loop at the end equals $4L\sqrt{gh}$ where L is lengths of basin and h is depth of basin, or $2L\sqrt{gh}$ for a partly closed entrances. $\sqrt{gh}$ is the propagation velocity of a translatory wave. This is a relatively frequent phenomenon in small Norwegian side fjords and in some oblong harbor basins.

Wave Rose

Port planning and layout, design, construction, and maintenance of coastal structure require a comprehensive knowledge and understanding of the wave condition.

In the stage of port planning, it is normally necessary to evaluate local wave conditions and summarize the statistics of wave height and directions. These data can be summarized in terms of wave rose. It is often very difficult to obtain the basic information needed for such analyses. Ideally, field data for such particular location under consideration should be known. To cover the necessary number of occurrences of sea conditions a minimum of 2～3 years of continued instrumental data collection is considered necessary.

Break Zone

When waves reach the beach with shallow water, they will break. There are three types of breakers: spilling, plunging, and surging. Spilling breakers tend to occur on beaches of very low slope with wave of high steepness values. The most dangerous type of wave breaking is the plunging when the wave crest travels faster than the wave as a whole. The front of the wave then begins to fall and finally develops a jet of water which strikes the base of the wave entrapping a pocket of air and throwing up a splash which typically rises as high as the crest elevation before plunging. Generally speaking suspended load transport in the breaker zone, due to breaking waves and the generated longshore currents. Breaker zone extends seaward

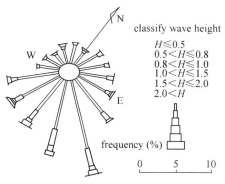

Figure 15-1　wave rose

from the shoreline to the break point. It is very important to know the breaker zone, when navigation channel, harbor basin, coastal structure are studied.

New Words and Expressions

1. harbor 港口,海港
2. maneuver 操纵
3. vessel 船,舰
4. mooring 下锚
5. berthing 停泊,泊位
6. navigation 通航
7. channel 航道
8. open-sea 外海
9. coast 海岸
10. long-period wave 长周期波,长波
11. critical limit 临界限制
12. beam sea 横浪
13. head sea 顶头浪
14. roll 横摇
15. yaw 首摇
16. couple 联结,耦合
17. penetration 穿透,传入
18. adverse effect 不良影响
19. eliminate 消除
20. resonance phenomenon 共振现象
21. wind wave 风浪
22. swell 涌浪
23. oscillation 振荡,振动
24. entrance 入口,口门
25. propagation 传播
26. velocity 速度
27. translatory wave 推进波
28. fjord 峡湾
29. oblong 长方形的,长椭圆形的

30. plan 规划

31. layout 布置

32. construction 施工

33. maintenance 维护

34. wave height 波高

35. direction 方向

36. in terms of 依据，按照

37. location 位置

38. instrumental 仪器的

39. break zone 破碎带，破碎区

40. spilling 崩破波

41. plunging 卷破波

42. surging 激散波

43. slope 坡度

44. steepness 陡度

45. wave crest 波峰

46. suspended load 悬疑质，悬荷

47. longshore current 沿岸流

48. seaward 向海的，朝海

49. shoreline 海岸线

50. break point 破波点

Lesson 16 Water Depth in Harbor

Water depth is one of the important technical characteristics in a port design, which should be sufficient for safe maneuvering and mooring of ships inside it. Generally, the larger water depth under the keel of ships which call at the port, the more convenient and safer conditions would be provided for ship's navigation. But unduly large water depth would increase the port's construction and maintenance costs. Therefore, an appropriate water depth would be for safe navigation of ships and not too much to cause extra costs. That means a suitable depth clearance should be defined.

Components of Water Depth Clearance and Determinants

When designing water depth, two main conditions should be considered for depth clearance:

(a) The minimum under-keel clearance for ships not to get aground when sailing or berthing;

(b) Clearance required for reducing the maneuvering difficulties of ships.

For the former condition, the factors resulting in the grounding of ships may include: (1) sounding error; (2) additional draught increased by ship movement. While the later should take account of two factors: one is depth clearance required for ship maneuvering, and the other is clearance needed to protect the cooling water opening for main engine's condenser from being blocked up. Figure 16 – 1 illustrates the above requirements.

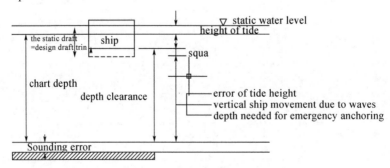

Figure 16 – 1 components of wave depth

Sounding Error and Barriers under Water

Change of water level. There lies difference between actual water level and measured one, which may result from tidal height measurement error or prediction error. The prediction error of water level is usual about 0.2 m, nevertheless, on the basis of the data of tidal observation from each port's tidal station, this kind of error could not be more than 0.01 – 0.02 m.

The chart measurement error. In accordance with the Code of Port Engineering Survey, it is defined that the tolerance error of chart is 0.5 m when the water depth is within 10 m; 0.2 m with water depth under 20 m, and 1/50 of water depth with water depth more than 20 m.

Clearance caused by anchor cast by ship. When a ship under sail needs to stop in emergency, it always drops its both-side anchors at the same time of running astern to help to come to a full stop. At this point, the casting anchors would act as barriers on the channel, and in this regard there should be under-keel clearance to avoid the anchors bumping into the ship's bottom. How much the anchor protrudes from the bottom depends on the anchor's type, weight, size and characteristics of bed materials etc(e.g. the anchors for a 100,000 DWT ship is about 13 tons, which would protrude out 1.3 m from the sea bottom at the emergency of anchoring).

New Words and Expressions

1. keel 龙骨
2. unduly 过度地
3. depth clearance 富余深度
4. result in 导致
5. grounding 搁浅
6. sounding error 探测误差
7. draught 吃水
8. condenser 冷凝器
9. tidal 潮汐的
10. observation 观测
11. tidal station 验潮站
12. tolerance error 容许误差

13. anchor 锚
14. cast 投掷
15. emergency 紧急情况
16. astern 向后，向船尾
17. protrude 突出

Lesson 17　Port Site Selection

The choice of a particular for the establishment of a port depends on many physical characteristics of the proposed port sites such as depth, available land areas, easy accessibility to the harbor and reliable protection of the harbor against wave action, current action, and sedimentation. The initial investment cost for a port development and future maintenance and dredging expenses may largely depend on the given physical characteristics of the proposed by port sites. In this section some of the major physical requirements that must be consider by port planners in choosing a port site are presented.

Basic Physical Criteria

In order for any location to be a good candidate for a port, a prerequisite is that it should be located in a sheltered area that is behind an island, in a deep natural bay, or in a sheltered lagoon or estuary.

The given site conditions affect not only the investment and maintenance costs as mentioned earlier but also the necessary requirements for safe operation of ships. The following environmental site conditions may impose some limit on the operation of ships:

(1) Astronomical tide and wind;

(2) Changes in water level (storm surges and the negative surges);

(3) Waves (direction, amplitude, height);

(4) Currents;

(5) Fog and ice.

A statistical survey of the site conditions mentioned earlier is necessary to estimate the maximum level of each condition and the frequency and duration of such occurrences. From this information the planners can evaluate the "operational limits" posed by each alternate site. The effects of the preceding environmental conditions on ships should be examined from a maneuvering as well as from an operational point of view while at berth.

The Requirement for General Developing

As mentioned before, most of the third generation ports owe the free business power which can attract multinational companies to enter the port area, increase the commercial transport amount, develop their business operation and provide huge number of cargo. So the port site should be selected to promote the implement and manage for the free trade policy conveniently, therefore, we'd better plan the port site, free duty area, export and import area synchronously.

The port site should be selected to attract the establishment of industrial area, provide more chances and conditions for urban and regional economic promotion.

The port site should not be selected to near the urban central line, besieged and crushed by urban accommodation area except for passenger transportation, but to be displaced to new port and mew urban region from the old urban region, to achieve the undisturbed regional structure and distribution.

A better port site should be in favor of present development and focus on development in the future too, e. g., 30 years reasonable developing.

The new port site should be coordinated with the original port district, and meet the new requirement. The new port site should be useful in exerting the comprehensive function of the new port and old port, make the old port valid in the larger and newer foundation.

The search for suitable locations for new port developments and for extensions to existing ports will be governed by the need for the following:

(1) Deep safe water at berthing points, and satisfactory approach channels.

(2) Sufficient land area.

(3) Good conveniently access to road, rail or waterway routes.

New Words and Expressions

1. establishment 建造,创办
2. proposed 被提议的,被推荐的
3. reliable 可靠的
4. current 水流
5. sedimentation 泥沙,沉降
6. dredge 疏浚
7. candidate 候选人,候补者
8. prerequisite 先决条件
9. sheltered area 被掩护区域

10. lagoon 泻湖
11. estuary 河口
12. investment 投资，投入
13. impose…on 施加影响于……
14. astronomical tide 天文潮
15. storm surge 风暴增水
16. negative surge 风暴减水
17. amplitude 振幅
18. duration 历时
19. besiege 围困，包围

Lesson 18　Classification of Terminals by Function

There are many classification methods of terminals, here we only introduce classification methods according to the function.

By the Cargo Type and Its Package

General cargo terminal. These are terminals equipped with conventional cranes, which handle cargo in all types of package compatible with cranes. The package could be parcels, sacks, pallets etc.

Multi-purpose terminal. These terminals combine a variety of functions in a single terminal, where containers, but also conventional general cargo, other packaged products or even heavy cargo, can be handled.

Container terminal. In this case, containers are handled using special loading and unloading, transferring and stacking equipment.

Ro-Ro terminal. Here cargo is transferred within a roll on-roll off system, with loading and unloading if cargo by horizontally moving lorries, forklifts, tractors, and so on.

Specialized terminal. Only one kind of cargo could be loaded or unloaded, such as coal-loading terminals, crude oil terminals etc.

By Trade Type

Terminals that primarily handling imported and exported cargo for foreign trade are called terminals for foreign trade; terminals that primarily handle imported and exported cargo for domestic trade are called terminals for domestic trade. When the cargo flow only has one dimension, the terminal is usually called export-oriented or the import-oriented terminal for foreign trade (or domestic trade).

By Its Ownership

Terminals which only serve for one company's or just a few companies' raw material or finished product are usually called dedicated terminals. This kind of terminals is usually invested by the factories and mines that use them. Terminals, invested by the Ministry of transport and serving the cargo owners of their hinterland, are public terminals. If many kinds of cargo could be handled there, we used to call this kind of terminals for general use.

By Serving Object

Terminals which mainly handle cargo are called cargo terminals, while the ones that serve the passengers are passenger terminals.

New Words and Expressions

1. classification 分类
2. terminal 终端,码头
3. according to 根据
4. genera cargo 杂货
5. crane 起重机
6. parcel 包
7. sack 麻袋,粗布袋
8. pallet 运货板
9. container 集装箱
10. horizontally 水平地
11. lorry 载货卡车
12. forklift 叉车
13. tractor 拖拉机
14. crude oil 原油
15. imported 进口的
16. exported 出口的
17. domestic 国内的
18. raw material 原材料
19. dedicated 专用的
20. mine 矿业
21. ministry 部
22. hinterland 腹地

Lesson 19　Layout of Breakwater

Nowadays, breakwaters at large water depth of more than 20 m are no more unusual in port construction. It results in the great influence on the site selection and the layout of a port because of the relatively high cost of breakwater construction. Therefore, in some ports, whether the lay of breakwaters is reasonable or not is of crucial importance in master plan of the port. Many factors affect the layout of breakwaters, such as natural conditions like winds, waves, currents, sediments, topography and geology, operational requirements, constructions investment etc. In the section, the principles of the breakwater layout are discussed.

Principles for Breakwater Layout

Layout of breakwaters should adapt to the berthing line, and meet the requirement of the tranquility of the harbor basin.

(1) Long period waves are dangerous to operation of ship handling and mooring. Those with period more than 30 s, or 1 minute, even if with small wave height, would cause great movement of mooring ships. Sometimes even result in the rupture of the mooring rope. Therefore, it should be carefully designed to avoid the resonance of water in harbor basin with the long period waves, and prevent the waves from penetrating through the breakwater.

(2) There should be adequate water area with sufficient depth protected by breakwaters for ship maneuvering, mooring and handling.

(3) A margin paid regard to the extreme limit of the development and ships with extreme dimensions which the port could accommodate as far as possible should be considered for port future development.

(4) The water area surrounded by breakwater should be well judged. It is not exactly good enough for larger area protected by the breakwaters. It must be kept in mind that if a harbor is too large, it may permit the generation of local waves within the harbor, which will make berthing difficult.

In ports at silty coastal area, it is easier for sediments which enter into the harbor mainly in suspension to deposit at calm water area. Therefore, the larger the water area and capacity to accept the tide of a port are, the greater volume of deposition would happen in it. From this point of view, the useless water area should be reduced as possible as one can to decrease the tide and sediments entering into port.

(5) It should be built on available advantageous grounds such as submerged reef, shoal, bar, and shallow water areas to save the investment as possible as it can.

New Words and Expressions

1. master plan 规划总图
2. topography 地形
3. geology 地质
4. adapt to 适应
5. tranquility 平静
6. harbor basin 港池
7. rupture 断裂
8. margin paid 保证金支付
9. accommodate 容纳
10. silty 淤泥的
11. deposit 沉积,沉淀
12. submerge 淹没
13. shoal 浅滩
14. bar 沙坝
15. shallow 浅水

Lesson 20   Fender

General

The marine fenders provide the necessary interface between the berthing ship and the berth structure, and therefore the principal function of the fender is to transform the impact load from the berthing ship into reactions which both the ship and berth structure can safely sustain. A properly designed fender system must therefore be able to gently stop a moving or berthing ship without damaging the ship, the berth structure or the fender. when the ship has berthed and been safely moored, the fender systems should be able and strong enough to protect the ship and the berth structure from the forces and motion caused by wind, waves current, tidal changes and loading or unloading of cargo. The design of fenders shall also take into account the importance of the consequences suffered by the ship and berthing structure in case of an eventual accident due to insufficient energy absorption capacity.

During design of berth and fender constructions in the past and even up to today, one has tended to plan and design the berth structure itself first, and only later the type of fender one hopes will satisfy the requirements as regards berth and ships. This approach to design has resulted in damages occurring quite frequently to berth and fender structures, and to a lesser degree to ships.

The correct procedure should be to plan and design the fender and berth structures jointly. The choice of fenders shall be dependent on the size of berthing ships and maximum impact energy. After having identified the fender's criteria, one can finalize the design of the berth superstructure. If the following factors are therefore considered in selecting the fender system:

(1) The fender system must have sufficient energy absorb capacity.

(2) The reaction force from the fender system dose not exceed the loading capacity of the berthing system.

(3) The pressure exerted from the fender system dose exceed the ship hull pressure capacity.

(4) The capital construction costs and maintenance costs are considered during the design of both the berth structure and fender system.

This procedure will lead to:

(1) Right structural solutions;

(2) Lower construction costs;

(3) Lower annual maintenance costs.

Fendering Requirements

A single or easy solution to the fender problems does not exist. Each type of berth structure has different demands. Factors having impact on the choice of fender are: size of ships, navigation methods, location, tidal differences, water depths, etc. A ship berthing along an exposed berth structure will obviously have other demands to the fender system than if it was to berth along a sheltered berth structure.

One can talk of a berth structure's "sensitivity" to impact from ships. Generally, a solid berth structure is more resistant to horizontal impact. Whereas an open berth structure is less resistant or more sensitive. This means that a berth structure's sensitivity to berthing impact increases with its "structural slenderness", and with increasing slenderness the fendering assumes greater importance. For instance, a berth structure of concrete blocks will be less vulnerable than e.g. an open-type pier supported by piles.

When selecting a fender system, one should bear in mind the purpose of the berth structure. Structures with special functions are usually provided with fender to accommodate certain types of ships, e.g. berths for old tankers. But on the other hand, if the berth should accommodate a large variation of ship sizes and types, e.g. a multi-purpose berth structure, the selection of fender system is far more difficult and will require detailed consideration and possibly special design treatment. The problem of selecting the right fender will be further complicated if the berth has an exposed location with difficult maneuvering conditions and/or is subjected to extreme tidal variation.

New Words and Expressions

1. fender 护舷
2. interface 交界面,接触面
3. transform 转变
4. impact load 撞击力
5. reaction 反作用

6. sustain 承受
7. tidal change 潮差
8. energy absorption 能量吸收
9. tend to 倾向于
10. frequently 频繁地
11. jointly 联合地
12. criteria 标准
13. finalize 最终确定
14. exceed 超过
15. ship hull 船体
16. sensitivity 敏感度
17. resistant 抵抗
18. slenderness 细长度
19. vulnerable 脆弱
20. pier 码头
21. pile 桩
22. oil tanker 油轮

Section IV Coastal Engineering

Lesson 21 Artificial Island

An artificial island is an island that has been constructed by humans rather than formed by natural processes. Such islands have been created by expanding existing islets, construction on existing reefs, or amalgamating several natural islets into a bigger island. Thus, they vary widely in size, from small islets reclaimed solely to support a single pillar, building, or other structure, to those that support entire communities.

Early artificial islands included floating structures in still waters and wooden or megalithic structures erected in shallow waters. In modern times, artificial islands have usually been formed by land reclamation, but some have been formed by the incidental isolation of an existing piece of land during canal construction, or by the flooding of valleys resulting in the tops of former knolls getting isolated by water. Some recent developments have been made more in the form of oil platforms, but there is disagreement whether they should be known as islands.

Artificial islands have been constructed for various purposes. In the past, some were built for ceremonial structures, and others were intended to isolate one group of people from another. More recently, they have been built to ease overcrowding in urban areas, accommodate airports, and promote tourism. In addition, there are proposals to build islands to mitigate coastal erosion or generate electric power from renewable energy sources. Critics, however, note that each project is extremely expensive and could potentially harm ecosystems.

The construction technologies of artificial island in China have been developed rapidly in recent 10 years. Only in Shengli Oilfield, the China's second largest oilfield, more than 20 artificial islands were so far completed.

Related Requirements for Construction & Employment of Artificial Island

(1) Soft Ground Treatment

Generally, the natural soft ground foundation for building an island in seabed needs to be treated and reinforced. There are a variety of soft ground foundation treatment methods, including removal and replacement, stabilization by dewatering and by consolidation, piling and caisson structure, and deep vibratory techniques and so on.

It is suggested that a comparing of different methods should be made based on both technological and economical factors.

(2) Storm Pavement and Apron

Due to the severe environmental conditions at beach-shallow sea, artificial island is always under attacks of varied forces such as sea wind, wave and water current, as well as ice etc.

It is very important for an island to lay storm pavement and apron to protect the island's slope, to ensure the island stability and safety, and to keep the filling materials inner the island not to be washout.

(3) Selections of Environmental Load

The main source of environmental loads such as sea wind, wave, ice accumulation etc. should be confirmed absolutely correct and precise, for they have considerable influence on project cost.

Specially, the confirmation of sea ice and earthquake loads must have enough data and evidence, for these two loads are the controlling ones on most cases.

(4) Observation and Inspection

It's necessary to observe and inspect the stability and strength of an artificial island during construction and employment in order to forecast possible accidents and reduce risks. Some monitoring instrument needs to be embedded inside the island during the construction period.

Normally, matters needed to be monitored include sedimentation of island foundation, displacement of component, sediment washing and remaining strength of structural component and materials.

(5) Safety and Lifesaving

It is obvious that lifesaving on the sea is exceptional important. Each artificial island must provide effective safe and lifesaving facilities and equipment, such as alarm device, rescue boat, fire fighting facilities and so on.

The emergency response plan must be proposed before the island being used.

Section IV Coastal Engineering

(6) Environment Protection

At the present, ocean environmental protection has been paid increasingly attention all over the world. For some possible pollution accident, there should be relevant prevention and treatment methods after the island being designed, constructed and employed.

In addition, some items should be evaluated before the project beginning. These items include environmental change during the period of island construction, environment influence due to the island employed, and environment harmfulness when the island being abandoned.

(7) Reuse the Caisson Components

Some components of the artificial island, e. g. caisson and bigger stones, are supposed to reuse time after time in order to reduce cost. This is also a development tendency of artificial island construction in the world.

Therefore, this factor ought to be thought over during the caisson's manufacture, transport, installation, removal and re-buildup, making the whole process simple, convenient and operated as easily as possible.

Generally, construction of an artificial island is of higher risk and needs higher investment; therefore the following requirements must be satisfied:

All national and international law and code involved ocean security and environmental protection must be abided.

The designing scheme should adopt advanced technology, reduce the cost, protect environment, ensure safety, and meet the needs of not only drilling and oil extraction, but also disassembly or moving after the island running down.

It is regarded that some principles should be followed when designing an island, such as adjusting measures to local conditions, taking advantage of nearby construction materials and convenience, shortening work time on the sea and so on.

New Words and Expressions

1. reef 礁石,暗礁
2. islet 小岛
3. pillar 柱子
4. reclamation 回收,再利用

5. erosion 侵蚀，腐蚀
6. ecosystem 生态系统
7. soft ground 软土地基
8. reinforce 加固，加强
9. dewater 使脱水，排水
10. consolidation 固结，巩固
11. pavement 铺砌层，面层
12. apron （防冲刷）护坦，码头前沿
13. sedimentation 沉降，沉淀
14. drilling and oil extraction 钻井和采油
15. disassembly 拆卸，分解

Lesson 22　FPSO

In recent years, offshore oilfield developments have been moving toward deeper water and more remote areas, and now these fields are located in water depths of over 5000 feet, which were once thought impracticable to develop economically. In addition, the fast diminishing rate of discovery of new giant fields, the so-called big elephants, necessitates the development of the smaller oil fields. The FPSO system is one concept that can lower the minimum economic field size, and make possible the development of these small or remote oil fields in deeper water.

As the abbreviation shows, the FPSO system has the functions of (Floating) Production, Storage, and Offloading. The FPSO system receives the fluid from the undersea oil reservoir via flexible risers through a turret mounted swivel, and the fluid is then separated to oil, gas, and water by the process equipment, and usually packaged into modules and secured on the deck of the vessel (production function). The separated oil is stowed in the vessel's tanks (storage function) for periodic offloading to a shuttle tanker (offloading function) using a floating hose arrangement. An FPSO system has production facilities on deck and large storage tanks in the hull.

In addition to these functions, the FPSO system has other functional components to ensure that the unit can be operated safely offshore. These components are the mooring system and turret that are required to keep on station, the riser system and swivel that are required to receive the fluid, and the safety and utility systems to support continuous operation offshore.

FPSO systems have several features that offer advantages in the development of a marginal oilfield, and these are itemized below:

Adaptability for Water Depth

Inherence in the nature of floating structures is their adaptability for a wide range of water depths. The concept of an FPSO system was introduced in 1974 in a water depth of 43 m, while today FPSO systems have been installed in water depths of 1,400 m. The cost increase for mooring an FPSO system in ultra-deep water (1,500 m – 3,000 m) is less than that for conventional fixed structures or tension leg platforms

(TLPs).

Early Deployment

The construction of FPSO systems, including the integration of process facilities, is carried out in shipyards, and is completed prior to leaving the shipyard. This approach minimizes the construction time since the fabrication of facilities is done in parallel with, and independently from, the construction or conversion of the vessel. If proper attention is paid to precommissioning, this also minimizes the commissioning phase at the offshore installation site. Therefore, the project cycle time (the period from project sanction to the first oil) is much shorter, and there is less risk of not keeping to the schedule than with fixed structures and with some TLPs that have to be mated near the shore or offshore.

Self-contained

As FPSO systems have an inbuilt storage capability in the cargo tanks, it is not necessary to build long, expensive pipelines to an existing infrastructure. Therefore, a remote oilfield, where there is no nearby pipeline network, can be developed by an FPSO system with minimum capital expenditure (CAPEX) and an enhanced project cycle time.

Movable and Relocatable

Once an oil reservoir is depleted, an FPSO system can easily be relocated to another field at less cost. This will only require disconnection of the riser and mooring systems. After minor modifications and/or dry-dock overhaul, the FPSO system can be installed in the next oilfield by connecting a newly installed mooring system. This feature gives a major financial advantage to the operator, as the capital cost of the vessel and its facilities can be allocated to several projects, which greatly enhances the economics of marginal fields.

Variable Combinations with Other Facilities

An FPSO or floating storage and offloading (FSO) system can be used with or without combination with other facilities such as a fixed wellhead platform, a subsea tree, TLPs, floating production systems (FPS), etc. Therefore, the FPSO system can be used for various field development options.

Crude Oil Market Expanded

With the use of FPSO system, there is the distinct advantage of being able to sell the crude oil to different markets, and thus being able to realize the best possible price for each barrel in current market conditions. The use of pipelines as the offtake mechanism often dictates where the product must be sold, and this is often at a lower price per barrel.

Segregated Storage

The cargo tanks in the FPSO system allow segregated storage of different crude oils from different oil wells on the same vessel, and thus might avoid the problems and price penalties associated with mixing crude of different quality. This is especially important when dealing with third-party production situations.

New Words and Expressions

1. offshore 离岸的,近海的
2. FPSO 浮式生产储油轮
3. TLP 张力腿平台
4. riser 立管
5. offtake 排水,输送
6. shuttle tanker 穿梭油轮
7. oil reservoir 油田,油池
8. segregated storage 分离存储

Lesson 23 Gravity-wall Structures

This type of structure can be subdivided into the following three groups depending on the type of structural design:

(1) block wall berths;

(2) caisson berths;

(3) cell berths.

The gravity berth wall structure may generally only be used where the seabed is good and the risk for settlement is low.

Block Wall Berths

Block wall berths belong to the oldest type of berth structures. They consist of large blocks placed one upon the other in a masonry wall pattern. Such berths, built on firm ground with blocks of good-quality natural stone or concrete, are structures of long life, and require only modest maintenance. Due to the present high costs of mining natural stone blocks, only concrete blocks can be considered economical for projects nowadays.

Due to many of newer ship types with strong bow thrusters, the erosion of the pitching in front of the wall structure has been a serious problem for many of the especially old block wall structures.

Since a great deal of the construction work has to be carried out under water by divers, the construction costs are usually very high. Only special local conditions could therefore justify the use of this type of structure nowadays. Such conditions could involve, for instance, a long berth to be founded on very firm ground, and, where cheap unskilled labor could be engaged, in casting a sufficient number of concrete blocks before the start of the actual construction. Thus any idle time for the skilled labor will be minimized. In order to minimize the extent of underwater work, the blocks should be of equal size, as far as possible, and, after casting the blocks, each course should first be arranged and marked onshore in order to facilitate its final placing in the water.

To ensure the stability of the individual blocks they should be sufficiently large that the maximum capacity of the block-handling equipment (cranes, etc.) is fully utilized.

Caisson Berths

In caisson quays the berth front is established by the placing of precast concrete caissons in a row corresponding to the planned alignment of the new berth. The caissons may be differently shaped and designed, depending on the site conditions and the available construction equipment. Rectangular caissons are the most usual.

The caissons are usually made ashore and then launched, towed out and sunk in position on a prepared gravel and/or rubble base. Thus, the underwater work is reduced to a minimum. It is both very economic and convenient if the caissons can be made on an existing slipway or in a dry dock, from which they can easily be launched. For economic reasons, the caissons should also preferably be made in a considerable number so that the production can be arranged in a rational way with multi-employment of the formwork units.

For convenience of construction, launching, towing, placing, etc. of the caissons, experience has shown that for economic reason the caisson dimensions should usually not be greater than about 30 m long, 25 m wide and 20 m high, but the concrete elements can be produced in a dry dock in lengths exceeding 100 m long. The caissons should be designed for all stages during construction and service.

The caissons are usually placed on a firm base of gravel and/or rubble, well compacted and accurately leveled. It is very important that before placing of the caissons, most of the settlements are brought to a minimum, particularly any uneven settlement. If the site is exposed to waves and currents, the base and the caissons should be designed in such a way that the time required for launching, towing and placing of the caissons is as short as possible. After placing of the caissons they are filled with suitable material, and a reinforced concrete cap is provided for the top, as is done on block wall berths.

In caisson berths it is easier to reduce the stresses at the outer edge of the caisson foot than is the case for block wall berths. Increasing the width of the caisson or providing it with two or three chambers of which only the rear chambers are filled, can reduce the stresses. The caissons must be designed to also resist the loads and stresses occurring during production, launching, towing, placing and filling.

All joints between the caissons must be sealed if the caissons are used to retain materials behind them and/or prevent waves or current from passing through the gaps between them. The joints should be designed for placing tolerances and uneven settlements. The placing tolerances should be 150 mm in sheltered water.

Cell Berths

During recent years sheet pile cell berths have become one of the most used types of gravity wall berth. One of the main reasons for this is the increasing ratio of the cost of labor to the cost of material, as compared to the construction of block wall and caisson berths. Various geometric configurations of sheet pile cell berths are used.

Circular main cells connected with arched cells are the most used form of construction. The circular cells have the advantage that each cell can be individually constructed and filled and are, therefore, independently stable.

Circular steel sheet pile cells with large diameters are one of the most used berth structures in the arctic, with ice-affected waters, since this type of berth structure can resist large horizontal forces.

The sheet pile cells offer the advantage that they can be designed as stable gravity walls without external anchoring. The nature of the cell fill material must be carefully specified and controlled. Experience has shown that the permeability of the sheet pile cells interlocking under tension is low, so the need for drainage through the cell constructions should be carefully investigated.

New Words and Expressions

1. berth 泊位,船台,造船滑道,箱位
2. caisson 沉箱,沉井
3. settlement 沉降
4. masonry 砌体,砌体工程,圬工
5. maintenance 维护,维修
6. bow thruster 船艏推进器
7. pitch 纵摇
8. crane 吊车,起重机
9. ashore 在岸上
10. launch 下水
11. tow out 拖运
12. slipway 滑道
13. dry dock 干船坞
14. tolerance 公差
15. permeability 渗透性,渗透率

Lesson 24　Harbor Basin

The harbor basin can be defined as the protected water area, which should provide safe and suitable accommodation for ships. Harbors can be classified as natural, semi-natural or artificial. Harbors have different functions, such as commercial harbors, refuge harbors, military harbors, oil harbors, etc.

Inside the harbor entrance, the harbor area should be allocated different functions such as berthing or turning area. If the harbor receives a wide range of ships, it should for economic reasons be divided into at least two zones, one for the larger and one for the smaller ships. The smaller ships should be located in the inner and shallower part of the harbor. Berths for hazardous cargoes such as oil and gas should be located at a safe distance and clearance from other berths. These activities should typically be located in isolated areas in the outer end and on the lee side of the harbor basin.

Entrance

The harbor entrance should, if possible, be located on the lee side of the harbor. If it must be located on the windward end of the harbor, adequate overlap of the breakwaters should be provided so that the ship will have passed through the restricted entrance and be free to turn with the wind before it is hit broadside by the waves.

Due to this overlap of the breakwaters the interior of the harbor will be protected from the waves. Accordingly, in order to reduce the wave height within the harbor, and to prevent strong currents, the entrance should be no wider than necessary to provide safe navigation.

The entrance width measured at the design depth will depend on the degree of wave protection required inside the harbor, the navigational requirements due to the size of ship, density of traffic, depth of water and the current velocity when the tide is coming in or going out.

Stopping Distance

The stopping distance of a ship will depend on factors such as ship speed, the displacement and shape of the hull, and horsepower ratio. The following stopping distances, as a rough guideline, are assumed to be sufficient to bring the ship to a complete halt. For ships in ballast, 3 – 5 times the ship's length is required. For a loaded ship, 7 to 8 times the ship's length is required.

Turning Area

The turning area or basin should usually be in the central area of the harbor basin. The size of the turning area will be a function of maneuverability and of the length of the ship using the area. It will also depend on the time permitted for the execution of the turning maneuver. The area should be protected from waves and strong winds. One should remember that ships in ballast have decreased turning performance.

The following minimum diameters of the turning area are generally accepted. The minimum diameter where the ship turns by going ahead and without use of bow thrusters and/or tugboat assistance should be approximately 4 times the length of the ship. Where the ship has tugboat assistance, the turning diameter could be 2 times the length of the ship. Under very good weather and maneuvering conditions these diameters might be reduced to 3 and 1.6 times the length respectively as a lower limit.

With use of the main propeller and rudder and the bow thrusters, the turning diameter could be 1.5 times the length of the ship.

Where the ship is turned by warping around a dolphin or pier and usually with tugboat assistance under calm conditions, the turning diameter could be a minimum 1.2 times the length of the ship.

New Words and Expressions

1. refuge 避难
2. hazardous cargo 危险品
3. windward 迎风向,上风向
4. entrance 口门
5. stopping distance 制动距离
6. turning area 回转水域
7. ballast 压载的

8. loaded 满载的

9. maneuverability 操控性

10. tugboat 拖轮

11. dolphin 靠船桩

Lesson 25　Hong Kong-Zhuhai-Macau Bridge

The Hong Kong-Zhuhai-Macao Bridge (HZMB), straddled across Lingdingyang of Pearl River Estuary, linking the Hong Kong Special Administrative Region (HKSAR), Zhuhai City of Guangdong Province and Macao Special Administrative Region. The total length is about 42km, counting from the Hong Kong Boundary Crossing Facilities at the east to the Zhuhai/Macao Boundary Crossing Facilities at the west. The uniqueness of the project includes:

(1) The HZMB will be the longest bridge-cum-tunnel sea-crossing with dual 3-lane carriageway, which is about 35.6 km in length from the shore of northern Lantau to the western shore of Pearl River Estuary.

(2) The HZMB is to be built with 120 years design life. The design and construction standard not only need to satisfy the requirements stated in Mainland's relevant regulations and the feasibility study report, but also suitably taking into account Hong Kong and Macao Standards.

(3) The HZMB construction environment is complicated. Frequent typhoons, crisscross navigation, airport height restrictions, high environmental standards, etc should be taken into considerations.

(4) To minimize the impact of the bridge design to river flow, navigation and hydrology, there is stringent requirement to control the water blockage ratio during the selection of options.

Using Large Span Sea Viaduct

The western sea viaduct will be composed of long span bridge sections with main spans in the range of 75 - 180 m. It passes over a navigation channel with a clearance of 41 m. Turnaround facility will be provided on this dual 3-lane highway for emergency and operational usages.

Adopting Specific Measures to Minimize Impacts to the Natural Environment

To the east of the sea viaduct section, the HKLR runs into the Airport Channel between the Hong Kong International Airport and the North Lantau. Several measures of the HKLR have been adopted to minimize disturbance to the existing natural environment. These include spanning over the headland between San Shek Wan and Sha Lo Wan of Lantau Island by adopting longer span lengths without physical contact with Lantau Island, minimizing the number of piers of viaduct portion at Sha Lo Wan to reduce visual impact, burying pile caps of the viaduct under the sea bed to minimize disturbance to the existing current flow of Airport Channel and shifting the viaduct to the Airport Island once the airport height restriction allows.

Provision of Landscaping Works for At-Grade Road

This 1.6 km at-grade road will run along the east coast of the Airport Island with provision of extensive landscaping works.

Formation of a Strategic Road Network

As an integral part of the HZMB project, HKLR will be connected effectively to the HZMB Main Bridge, the nearby Hong Kong International Airport, as well as the Tuen Mun and North Lantau area, to form a strategic road network to achieve overall effectiveness and efficiency in land transportation.

The non-dredge Reclamation Method

Conventionally, seawalls are constructed on firm foundations by replacing the soft marine mud in the seabed by sand fill. This process requires dredging and dumping of a large amount of soft marine mud.

With a view to minimizing the environmental impacts caused by the dredging and dumping for reclamation, Highways Department has developed a non-dredge reclamation for reclaiming the 150 ha artificial island for the HKBCF (including about 20 ha of land for Southern Landfall of Tuen Mun-Chek Lap Kok Link) from the open waters off the northeast of the Hong Kong International Airport. This is the first time this new construction method is used in Hong Kong.

Part of the seawall of the artificial island will be formed by sinking large diameter circular steel cells through the soft marine mud. The steel cells will then be filled up by inert construction and demolition material or sand.

The adoption of the above non-dredge reclamation will greatly reduce the amount of dredging and dumping of marine mud by about 22 Mm^3, and will also reduce the use of about one half of the backfilling material. Furthermore, there will be less impact to the water quality and a large reduction in the construction marine traffic during construction of the reclamation works. This will help to preserve the marine ecology especially the Chinese White Dolphins habitat.

The non-dredge reclamation has lots of benefits over the conventional dredge seawall construction method, including:

(1) Reduce dredging and disposal of marine mud by about 97%;
(2) Reduce backfilling material by about one half;
(3) Reduce suspended particles by about 70%;
(4) Reduce construction marine traffic by about one half.

Adoption of Tunnel Boring Machines for the Construction of the Sub-sea Tunnel

Construction of the proposed sub-sea tunnel across the Urmston Road between HKBCF and Tuen Mun is proposed to be built by two approximately 14 m diameter Tunnel Boring Machines (TBMs). The use of TBM to form the proposed sub-sea tunnels saves the need of dredging and disposal of some 11 Mm^3 of marine sediment that would otherwise be required by traditional immersed tube method.

The adoption of TBM also saves the need to divert several existing power cables now serving the HKIA, minimizes the impact on the busy Urmston Road during construction and the impacts to the marine habitat of the Chinese White Dolphin, within and near the works area of the project. The use of large diameter TBMs of this size to build a sub-sea tunnel in Hong Kong is unprecedented and will be a great challenge to the construction industry in Hong Kong.

New Words and Expressions

1. estuary 河口
2. bridge-cum-tunnel 桥隧工程
3. sea-crossing 跨海的
4. feasibility study 可行性研究
5. taking into account/consideration 考虑
6. typhoon 台风
7. dredge 疏浚,浚挖
8. backfill 回填
9. suspend 悬浮

Lesson 26 Spar

A spar is a type of floating oil platform typically used in very deep waters, and is named for logs used as buoys in shipping that are moored in place vertically. Spar production platforms have been developed as an alternative to conventional platforms. The deep draft design of spars makes them less affected by wind, wave and currents and allows for both dry tree and subsea production.

A spar platform consists of a large-diameter, single vertical cylinder supporting a deck. The cylinder is weighted at the bottom by a chamber filled with a material that is more dense than water to lower the center of gravity of the platform and provide stability. Additionally, the spar hull is encircled by helical strakes to mitigate the effects of vortex-induced motion. Spars are permanently anchored to the seabed by way of a spread mooring system composed of either a chain-wire-chain or chain-polyester-chain configuration.

There are three primary types of spars: the classic spar, truss spar, and cell spar. The classic spar consists of three sections. The upper section is compartmentalized around a flooded centerwell containing the different type of risers. This section provides the buoyancy for the spar. The middle section is also flooded but can be economically configured for oil storage. The bottom section is compartmentalized to provide buoyancy during transport and to contain any field-installed, fixed ballast.

A truss spar has a shorter cylindrical "hard tank" than a classic spar and has a truss structure connected to the bottom of the hard tank. This truss structure consists of four large orthogonal "leg" members with X-braces between each of the legs and heave plates at intermediate depths to provide damping. At the bottom of the truss structure, there is a relatively small keel, or soft tank, that houses the heavy ballasting material. Soft tanks are typically rectangular in shape but have also been round to accommodate specific construction concerns. The majority of spars are of this type.

A third type of spar, the cell spar, has a large central cylinder surrounded by smaller cylinders of alternating lengths. At the bottom of the longer cylinders is the soft tank housing the heavy ballasting material, similar to a truss spar. The cell spar design was only ever used for one platform, the Red Hawk spar, which was decommissioned in 2014 under the Bureau of Safety and Environmental Enforcement's "Rigs-to-Reefs" program. At the time of its decommissioning it was the deepest floating platform to ever be decommissioned.

Oil and gas exploration in deep water has accelerated the need of ocean structures suitable for these depths. A spar platform is such a compliant floating structure used for deep water for the drilling, production, processing and storage of ocean deposits. The follows gives a review on the technical development of spar platform, including the research on dynamic response, mooring system, fatigue and coupled analysis and the design of heave plate and strake configuration.

The Spar may be more economical to build for small and medium sized rigs and has more inherent stability than a TLP since it has a large counterweight at the bottom and does not depend on the mooring to hold it upright. It also has the ability, because of the small waterline area and by use of chain-jacks attached to the mooring lines, to move horizontally over the oil field.

After the onshore assembly the hull is transported to the destination and then the crane barge up-end the hull. While the hull is being held loosely in place, the pump boat fills the hull's lower ballast tank and floods the centerwell to make the hull self-up-end. Next, the derrick barge lifts into place a temporary work deck which acts as basic utility hook up, mooring line attachment, and riser installation.

The hull is positioned on location by a tug and positioning system assistance. Then the mooring system is connected to the hull. After the mooring system is connected, the lines are pretensioned. Then the hull is ballasted to prepare for the topsides installation and removal of the temporary work deck.

Topsides are transported offshore on a material barge and lifted into place by the derrick barge.

The last pieces of equipment to be installed are buoyancy cans and the associated stems. The cans are simply lifted off the material barge and placed into slots inside the centerwell bay. Next, the stems are stabbed onto the cans.

New Words and Expressions

1. Spar 单立柱平台
2. Classic spar 经典式 Spar
3. Truss spar 桁架式 Spar
4. Cell spar 集束式 Spar
5. chamber 房间,室
6. vortex-induced motion 涡激运动
7. fatigue and coupled analysis 疲劳和耦合分析的研究
8. heave plate 垂荡板
9. buoyancy can 浮力舱
10. centerwell 中心井

Section Ⅴ Specification and Contract

Lesson 27 Choice of Structure

1. General

For any important structure, a variety of different types should be compared and a choice made on the basis of the capital and maintenance costs or ease of construction. The use of standardized designs to meet various conditions may not be economic. The typical designs given in this code are not intended to exclude the use of alternative structural arrangements, including hybrids of two or more of the arrangements described.

2. Types of Structure

Maritime structures can be either solid or open-piled. An open-piled structure can be either rigid or flexible.

Solid structures include all sheet and gravity walls with a solid vertical berthing face. These types of structure are most commonly used for marginal berths where fill material has to be retained, but they are also used for finger piers, jetties and dolphins.

Open structures have a suspended deck supported on piles. The structure can be either flexible with only vertical piles and without external horizontal restraint or constructed more rigidly with raking piles or with struts to the shore. The degree of flexibility will depend on the overall configuration, framing and relative stiffness of members and their supports. A flexible type of structure may be unsuitable if it is to accommodate cranes or bulk handling equipment, especially in earthquake zone.

Many types of quay structure that retain the ground behind them yield slightly during or after construction, with the development of active soil pressure and passive resistance. Yielding may take the form of horizontal movement or a horizontal movement combined with a forward rotation. These movements are in addition to natural settlements and will depend on the type of structure and the ground conditions. The effect of such movements on fixed superstructures that span from a support on the quay structure or from retained ground within the active wedge to another support on the ground remote from it, should be considered. The proximity of existing structures should be taken into account when selecting the type of structure to be adopted for a new quay. Changes to the existing maritime regime at the berth and at adjacent locations are likely to be smaller for open-piled than for solid structures, as they present less obstruction to current flow and waves. At sites where siltation is likely to occur, a solid structure may increase current velocities, thereby reducing the volume of material deposited alongside, but possibly causing adverse effects elsewhere. A solid structure can cause unacceptable disturbances for a ship at berth, due to reflected waves, but this may be reduced by the provision of perforations or a partly open face. Where open structures are used for marginal berths, the back-of-berth fill is usually retained behind a reveted slope. This slope can be used to absorb wave energy and reduce reflection.

The spring energy of a flexible structure can be used to absorb some or all of the energy of a berthing vessel.

Whatever the type of structure, its design should be sufficiently tolerant for it to accommodate local variations in site conditions which may be encountered during construction.

3. Seabed Conditions

The geotechnical data and bathymetric survey should be studied together to determine suitable founding levels for different types of structure and to decide if dredging is necessary or economic.

4. Local Construction Materials

Included in any geotechnical survey should be a study of the locally available natural materials for construction. The availability of rock or general fill within a short haul distance may have a strong influence on the choice of structure.

5. Method of Construction

The method and sequence of construction and availability of major construction plant may determine the type of structure finally selected. The maximum use of prefabricated sections may be adopted to achieve an early completion date, but the size and weight of units have to be within the handling capacity of available plant. When the facility is part of a large project, a design involving the mobilization of specialized equipment and the establishment of a large fabrication plant for the project as a whole may have cost advantages. Construction from on shore by the creation of a temporary bund, or a construction which works progressively forward from the shoreline or on a jack-up pontoon may be necessary if the weather conditions are too rough for the use of floating plant, either throughout the year or seasonally.

6. Construction Difficulties

The design should make allowance for the fact that the structure will generally be constructed over water from temporary working platforms. Fast currents and wave action will increase the difficulty of accurate construction. The tolerances normal in building work on land often cannot be achieved in these conditions. In particular, it should be remembered that a pile driven over water is seldom supported over its full length and, although it may be correctly located on the seabed, the head may deviate from the correct position. Deck units to be placed on piles should be designed to accommodate the permissible deviation in the piles. Excavation on land can be carefully controlled but under water it has to be executed by dredger or occasionally by diver. Dredgers will leave an undulating or stepped surface on which a layer of fine material may be deposited. It should be remembered that overdredging tolerances (typically 0.3 m in sand, silt and soft clay) can often be exceeded and that any pockets may fill with soft material. The unevenness of cut which is usually obtained and the possibility of the surface layer forming a potential failure plane under foundations should be considered. A layer of gravel or rubble may be placed on the seabed prior to filling to prevent the formation of such a failure plane below fill. Temporary slopes on which soft material may build up should be formed with an inclination opposite to that of the potential failure planes in the soil.

When precast units are to be placed on a gravel bedding layer on the seabed, the final levelling and preparation of the bedding has to be carried out by divers, often with poor visibility. As far as possible divers' work should be kept simple.

Adequate protection of the works during construction should be provided to avoid damage caused by floating craft, waves and currents.

New Words and Expressions

1. open-piled structure 透空桩基结构
2. marginal berth 顺岸泊位
3. finger pier 突堤码头
4. jetty 栈桥
5. dolphin 系靠船墩
6. raking pile 斜桩
7. bulk handling equipment 散货装卸设备
8. geotechnical data 地质资料
9. bathymetric survey 水深测量
10. dredging 疏浚
11. prefabricated sections/precast unit 预制构件
12. temporary bund 临时堤
13. jack-up pontoon 顶升趸船
14. excavation 挖掘
15. undulating 波状的
16. make allowance for 顾及;考虑
17. prior to 在……之前

Notes

1. For any important structure, a variety of different types should be compared and a choice made on the basis of the capital and maintenance costs or ease of construction.

建造任何重要结构之前,宜首先比较各种不同的型式,然后根据基建资金和维修费用或施工难易程度做出合适的选择。

此句为并列句,前一句的主语是 a variety of different types,后一句的主语是 a choice, a choice 后面省略了 should be。on the basis 是介词短语,作方式状语,修饰动词 made,意为"根据……做出选择"。

2. These types of structure are most commonly used for marginal berths where fill material has to be retained, but they are also used for finger piers, jetties and dolphins.

这种结构最常使用于必须挡住填筑材料的顺岸泊位,但这种结构也常用于突堤码头、栈桥和系靠船墩。

句中 where fill material has to be retained 是 where 引导的定语从句,修饰 marginal berths,意为"必须挡住填筑材料的顺岸泊位"。

3. Changes to the existing maritime regime at the berth and at adjacent locations are likely to be smaller for open-piled than for solid structures, as they present less obstruction to current flow and waves.

在泊位处和邻近地点,透空桩基结构使目前海洋规律发生的变化很可能要小于实体结构引起的变化,这是因为透空桩基结构对潮流和波浪的阻力相对较小。

此句的主干是 Changes are likely to be smaller。"to the existing maritime regime"是介词短语作后置定语,修饰 changes,意为"使目前海洋规律发生的变化"。"at the berth and at adjacent locations"是介词短语作地点状语,修饰 changes,意为"在泊位处和邻近地点发生的变化"。句中是对两种变化做了对比,一种是 open-piled structures 引起的变化,一种是 solid structures 引起的变化,for open-piled structures 和 for solid structures 均修饰主语 changes,意为"透空桩基结构使目前海洋规律发生的变化"和"实体结构使目前海洋规律发生的变化"。从 be smaller than 可以看出,透空桩基结构使其发生的变化要小于实体结构使其发生的变化。"as"引导原因状语从句,解释了原因。

4. At sites where siltation is likely to occur, a solid structure may increase current velocities, thereby reducing the volume of material deposited alongside, but possibly causing adverse effects elsewhere.

在易发生淤积的地方,实体结构可使海水流速增快,从而减少岩结构的淤积量,但很可能对其他地方带来不利影响。

此句的主干是 a solid structure may increase velocities。At sites…是整个主句的地点状语。where siltation is likely to occur 是后置定语从句,修饰 sites,意为"在易发生淤积的地方"。thereby reducing, but causing 是现在分词引导的结果状语,but 是用来引导表示转折的并列句。deposited alongside 为后置定语,deposited 前面省略了 which was,修饰 material,意为"岩结构的淤积物"。

5. Construction from on shore by the creation of a temporary bund, or a construction which works progressively forward from the shoreline or on a jack-up pontoon may be necessary if the weather conditions are too rough for the use of floating plant, either throughout the year or seasonally.

如果全年或季节性地使用浮动机具时,天气条件都太坏,可能有必要在岸上建一临时堤进行施工,也可从岸线开始向前逐步施工或在顶升趸船上施工。

Section V　Specification and Contract

此句主干是 construction or a construction may be necessary. 意为"有必要……进行施工,也可……施工。"from on shore 是介词短语作地点状语,by the creation of a temporary bund 是介词短语作方式状语,均修饰 construction,意为"在岸上建一临时堤进行施工"。which works progressively forward 是定语从句,修饰第二个 construction,意为"向前逐步进行的施工"。from the shoreline or on a jack-up pontoon 是地点状语,修饰动词 work,or 表示选择关系,意为"可从岸线开始向前逐步施工,也可在顶升趸船上施工"。if 引导条件状语从句,意为"如果"。either throughout the year or seasonally 是时间状语。翻译时,将名词性的 the use 转换成动词"使用"比较合适,即"全年或季节性地使用浮动机具"。

Lesson 28 Loads

1. General

Reference should be made to section five of BS 6349: Part 1: 1984 for the loads and soil pressures and to section six of BS 6349: Part 1: 1984 for the hydrostatic forces to which a maritime structure is subjected. For fendering and mooring systems, reference should be made to BS 6349: Part 4.

Loads can be grouped under the general headings given in 3.2.2 for the initial design but it may be necessary to consider the loads within a group separately when they are unusual or of particular significance.

2. Types of Load

(1) **Dead load.** The dead load is the effective weight of the structural elements of the structure. For some design analyses it may be preferable to consider the weight of the elements in air and to treat the uplift due to hydrostatic forces separately. This may be particularly important when considering the effect of artesian water.

(2) **Superimposed dead load.** The superimposed dead load is the weight of all materials forming loads on the structure that are not structural elements. Typical examples are the fill material on a relieving platform, surfacing, fixed equipment for cargo handling and quay furniture. The self-weight of large, slow-moving cranes on fixed tracks, such as container cranes, may be included in this category. In any analysis the effect of removing the superimposed dead load has to be considered, since it may diminish the overall stability or diminish the relieving effect on another part of the structure.

(3) **Live loads.** Live loads are subdivided in 47.2 of BS 6349: Part 1: 1984 into the following categories:

① cyclic;

② impulsive;

③ random;

④ static and long-term cyclic.

The first three categories are dynamic loads and it may be necessary to consider them separately to calculate the response of the structure.

Cyclic and random loads are mostly environmental but cyclic loading can be caused by vibrations from traffic or machinery.

The position and combinations of the live static and long term cyclic loads should be chosen so that their damaging effect on the structure is the most severe.

(4) **Soil and differential water loads.** Soil and differential water loads are the dominant loads affecting the stability of an earth-retaining structure. The disturbing forces are affected by the surcharge and live loads on the retained soil.

(5) **Environmental loads.** Because of their long term nature, environmental loads, such as the effects of snow, ice, temperature, current, tide and time-averaged wind, are not considered as dynamic loads.

Cyclic loads are induced by regular wave trains and vortex shedding in steady currents. Wave slam forces are considered as impulsive loads, while random loads include direct wave loads, wave-induced loads, seismic loading and turbulent wind loads.

3. Load Combinations for Overall Stability

(1) **General.** The loading conditions given in 3.2 to 3.4 should not be considered as exclusive, and any other critical conditions which might possibly occur should also be analysed. Although some combinations of loads are mutually exclusive, the probability of two or more large loads being applied to the structure simultaneously should be assessed. Depending on the consequences of failure, in most cases, it will not be economic to design for the simultaneous application of all possible extreme loads. However, where there is a very low probability that two large loads will occur simultaneously, the structure may be analysed using reduced factors of safety.

(2) **Normal loading conditions.** Normal loading refers to any combination of loads that may reasonably be expected to occur during the design life of the structure, associated with normal operating conditions. This should include any foreseeable modifications to the structure, earthworks, paving, storage patterns, handling equipment or dredged depth.

The maximum normal value of each type of load should be considered in combination, having regard to the provisions of 3.1. Examples of normal loading conditions are:

① overdredging of seabed within specified tolerances;

② increase in hydrostatic head due to drawdown in an impounded basin occurring during planned inspections at intervals not exceeding 1 year;

③ water levels in the tide range mean high water springs (MHWS) to mean low water springs (MLWS);

④ environmental loads that generally have a return period of 1 year or that impose restrictions on port operations, but excluding earthquakes and tsunamis;

⑤ normal berthing operations as described in BS 6349: Part 4;

⑥ loads derived from average soil properties in accordance with BS 8002;

⑦ loads due to containers, using diversification factors for stacks more than one container high.

(3) Extreme loading conditions. Extreme loading refers to any combination of loads that may be expected to occur during the design life of the structure, associated with the most severe credible load that could physically be applied, excluding accidental loads, such as that due to an uncontrolled berthing. The likelihood of more than one extreme load occurring at any time should be assessed. The secondary effects of such a load on other types of load, for example, the effect on soil properties of earthquakes or flooding, should be carefully considered.

However, the possibility of long term changes in conditions, such as deterioration of drainage systems, which could apply during application of the most credible load, should also be considered. Examples of extreme loading conditions are:

① deepening of the seabed due to scour;

② an increase in the hydrostatic head due to drawdown in an impounded basin occurring as a result of occasional inspections or accidental damage to gates;

③ astronomical water levels outside the tide range for normal loading conditions;

④ environmental loads with a return period equal to the design life of the structure;

⑤ abnormal berthing operations, as described in BS 6349: Part 4;

⑥ loads derived from the upper or lower quartile of soil properties, whichever is the more severe;

⑦ loads due to containers without the use of diversification factors;

⑧ earthquakes and tsunamis.

(4) Temporary loading during construction. The loads that may be expected to be applied at each stage of construction should be carefully considered.

New Words and Expressions

1. hydrostatic forces 静水压力
2. mooring systems 系泊设施
3. dead load 恒载
4. artesian water 承压水
5. live loads 可变荷载
6. soil and differential water loads 土和剩余水荷载
7. dynamic loads 动荷载
8. cyclic loads 周期荷载
9. mean high water springs (MHWS)大潮平均高潮位
10. mean low water springs (MLWS)大潮平均低潮位
11. credible load 可靠荷载
12. be subjected to 承受,受到
13. be preferable to 最好
14. at intervals 不时,相隔一段时间

Notes

1. Loads can be grouped under the general headings given in 3.2.2 for the initial design but it may be necessary to consider the loads within a group separately when they are unusual or of particular significance.

初步设计时,可按 3.2.2 中所给的总标题将荷载分组,但在不寻常或极其关键的情况下,则应分别考虑组内各种荷载。

此句为 but 引导的并列句。句中 under the general headings 是介词短语作条件状语,修饰前面的主句 Loads can be grouped,意为:"可按总标题将荷载分组"。given in 3.2.2 for the initial design 是过去分词短语作后置定语,修饰 headings,意为:"3.2.2 中所给的总标题"。when 引导条件状语从句,修饰 consider,意为"但在不寻常或极其关键的情况下,则应分别考虑……"。

2. The superimposed dead load is the weight of all materials forming loads on the structure that are not structural elements.

附加恒载是建筑物上形成荷载的全部材料的重量,而非结构构件的重量。

此句的主干是 The superimposed dead load is the weight of all materials。

forming loads 是现在分词短语作定语，修饰 materials，意为"形成荷载的全部材料"。on the structure 是介词短语作地点状语，修饰 forming，意为"在建筑物上形成荷载"。that 引导定语从句，修饰 materials，意为"非结构构件的材料"。

3. In any analysis the effect of removing the superimposed dead load has to be considered, since it may diminish the overall stability or diminish the relieving effect on another part of the structure.

由于移去附加恒载可能会降低整体稳定性或削弱作用在结构另一部分上的卸荷效果，因此在任何分析中都宜考虑移去附加恒载造成的影响。

此句的主干是 the effect of removing the superimposed dead load has to be considered。in any analysis 是介词短语作整个句子的条件状语，意为："在任何分析中，都宜考虑……"。since 引导原因状语从句，意为"因为，由于"。

4. The position and combinations of the live static and long term cyclic loads should be chosen so that their damaging effect on the structure is the most severe.

设计时，宜选择可变静荷载和永久周期荷载对结构破坏性最严重的位置和组合。

此句的主干是 The position and combinations of the live static and long term cyclic loads should be chosen。so that 引导结果状语从句，意为"使可变静荷载和永久周期荷载对结构的破坏最严重"。

5. The loading conditions given in 3.2.3.2 to 3.2.3.4 should not be considered as exclusive, and any other critical conditions which might possibly occur should also be analysed.

3.2.3.2 和 3.2.3.4 中给出的荷载情况并不是唯一的，也宜分析可能发生的其他任何一种临界情况。

此句为并列句。前句的主语是 the loading conditions，given in 3.2.3.2 to 3.2.3.4 是过去分词短语作后置定语，修饰 conditions，意为"3.2.3.2 和 3.2.3.4 中给出的荷载情况"。consider…as…是固定搭配，意为："认为……是……"。后句的主语是 any other critical conditions，which might possibly occur 是后置定语，修饰主语 any other critical conditions，意为"可能发生的其他任何一种临界情况"。

Lesson 29 Design

1. General Design Obligations

The Contractor shall be deemed to have scrutinized, prior to the Base Date, the Employer's Requirements (including design criteria and calculations, if any). The Contractor shall be responsible for the design of the Works and for the accuracy of such Employers Requirements (including design criteria and calculations), except as stated below.

The Employer shall not be responsible for any error, inaccuracy or omission of any kind in the Employer's Requirements as originally included in the Contract and shall not be deemed to have given any representation of accuracy or completeness of any data or information, except as stated below. Any data or information received by the contractor, from the Employer or otherwise, shall not relieve the contractor from his responsibility for the design and execution of the Works.

However, the Employer shall be responsible for the correctness of the following portions of the Employer's Requirements and of the following data and information provided by (or on behalf of) the Employer:

(1) portions, data and information which are stated in the Contract as being immutable or the responsibility of the Employer,

(2) definitions of intended purposes of the Works or any parts thereof,

(3) criteria for the testing and performance of the completed Works, and

(4) portions, data and information which cannot be verified by the Contractor, except as otherwise stated in the Contract.

2. Contractor's Documents

The Contractor's Documents shall comprise the technical documents specified in the Employer's Requirements, documents required to satisfy all regulatory approvals, and the documents described in Sub-Clause 5.6 [As-Built Documents] and Sub-Clause 5.7 [Operation and Maintenance Manuals]. Unless otherwise stated in the Employer's Requirements, the Contractor's Documents shall be written in the language for communications defined in Sub-Clause 1.4 [Law and Language].

The Contractor shall prepare all Contractor's Documents, and shall also prepare any other documents necessary to instruct the Contractor's Personnel.

If the Employer's Requirements describe the Contractor's Documents which are to be submitted to the Employer for review, they shall be submitted accordingly, together with a notice as described below. In the following provisions of this Sub-Clause, (1) "review period" means the period required by the Employer for review, and (2) "Contractor's Documents" exclude an documents which are not specified as being required to be submitted for review.

Unless otherwise stated in the Employer's Requirements, each review period shall not exceed 21 days, calculated from the date on which the Employer receives a Contractor's Document and the Contractor's notice. This notice shall state that the Contractor's Document is considered ready, both for review in accordance with this Sub-Clause and for use. The notice shall also state that the Contractor's Document complies with the Contract, or the extent to which it does not comply.

The Employer may within the review period, give notice to the Contractor that a Contractor's Document fails (to the extent stated) to comply with the Contract. If a Contractor's Document so fails to comply, it shall be rectified, resubmitted and reviewed in accordance with this Sub-Clause, at the Contractor's cost.

For each part of the Works, and except to the extent that the Parties otherwise agree:

(1) execution of such part of the Works shall not commence prior to the expiry of the review periods for all the Contractor's Documents which are relevant to its design and execution;

(2) execution of such part of the Works shall be in accordance with these Contractor's Documents, as submitted for review; and

(3) if the Contractor wishes to modify any design or document which has previously been submitted for review, the Contractor shall immediately give notice to the Employer. Thereafter, the Contractor shall submit revised document to the Employer in accordance with the above procedure.

Any such agreement (under the proceeding paragraph) or any review (under this Sub-Clause or other-wise) shall not relieve the Contractor from any obligation or responsibility.

3. Contractor's Undertaking

The Contractor undertakes that the design, the Contractor's Documents, the execution and the completed works will be in accordance with:

(1) the Laws in the Country, and

(2) the documents forming the Contract, as altered or modified by Variations.

4. Technical Standards and Regulations

The design, the Contractor's Document, the execution and the completed Works shall comply with the country's technical standards, building, construction and environmental Laws, Laws applicable to the product being produced from the Works, and other standards specified in the Employer's Requirements, applicable to the Works, or defined by the applicable Laws.

All these Laws shall, in respect of the Works and each Section, be those prevailing when the Works or Section are taken over by the Employer under Clause 10 [Employer's Taking Over]. References in the Contract to published standards shall be understood to be references to the edition applicable on the Base Date, unless stated otherwise.

If changed or new applicable standards come into force in the country after the Base Date, the Contractor shall give notice to the Employer and (if appropriate) submit proposals for compliance. In the event that:

(1) the Employer determines that compliance is required, and

(2) the proposals for compliance constitute a variation, then the Employer shall initiate a variation in accordance with Clause 13 [Variations and Adjustments].

New Words and Expressions

1. Contractor 承包商
2. Base Date 基准日期
3. Employer's Requirements 雇主要求
4. Sub-Clause 款
5. Clause 条
6. notice n. 通知
7. otherwise 除非。"合同双方另有协议",可以说"the Parties otherwise agree"。unless otherwise 意为"除非",比"if"和"otherwise"表达正式。该词组由两个同义词"unless"和"otherwise"组成,一般后面紧跟动词,意为"除非另……"。比如表示"除非合同另有规定",可以说 "unless otherwise stated/specified in the Contract"。
8. thereof: of that, of it 由此;其。在表示已提及的"人或事……"时,为避免重复,可使用该词,比如表示"合同条件、条款"时,可以说"the terms, conditions than provisions thereof",这里 thereof 意为"of the contract"。又如表示"工程任何部分",可说"any parts thereof",这里 thereof 意为 "of the Works"。

9. including design criteria and calculations, if any 包括设计标准和计算,如果有

10. except as stated below 除下述情况外

11. relieve the contractor from his responsibility 解除承包商承担的职责

12. be deemed 被认为

13. in accordance with/ under 根据,按照

14. applicable to 适用于

15. in respect of 关于

16. in the event that/in the event of 如果,如果……发生(比 when 正式)

Notes

1. The Employer shall not be responsible for any error, inaccuracy or omission of any kind in the Employer's Requirements as originally included in the Contract and shall not be deemed to have given any representation of accuracy or completeness of any data or information, except as stated below.

除下述情况外,雇主不应对原包括在合同内的雇主要求中的任何错误、不准确、或遗漏负责,并不应被认为,对任何数据或资料给出了任何准确性或完整性的表示。

句中 as originally included in the Contract 中的 as 作连词,引导状语从句,构成省略形式"as + 过去分词"这一特殊结构,译成汉语时作用如定语,修饰 any error, inaccuracy or omission,意为"原包括在合同内的任何错误、不准确或遗漏"。In the Employer's Requirements 是介词短语作定语,也修饰 any error, inaccuracy or omission,意为"雇主要求中的任何错误、不准确或遗漏"。此句有两个并列谓语"shall not be responsible"和"shall not be deemed"。be deemed to 意为"被认为是"。"except as stated below"是介宾短语,充当让步状语,修饰整个句子,意为"除下述情况外,雇主不应……,并不应……"。

2. If the Employer's Requirements describe the Contractor's Documents which are to be submitted to the Employer for review, they shall be submitted accordingly, together with a notice as described below.

如果雇主要求中描述了要提交雇主审核的承包商文件,这些文件应依照要求,连同下文叙述的通知一并上报。

句子主干是 they shall be submitted。句中 which are to be submitted to the

Employer 是定语从句，修饰 Contractor's Documents，for review 是介词短语作目的状语，修饰 submitted，意为"提交雇主，为了审核的承包商文件"。If 引导条件状语从句，修饰整个句子，意为"如果……，这些文件应……"。accordingly 相当于 according to the the Contractor's Documents。together with a notice 意为"连同通知一并"，as described below 修饰 notice，意为"下文叙述的通知"。

3. Unless otherwise stated in the Employer's Requirements, each review period shall not exceed 21 days, calculated from the date on which the Employer receives a contractor's Document and the Contractor's notice.

除非雇主要求中另有说明，每项审核期不应超过 21 天，从雇主收到一份承包商文件和承包商通知的日期算起。

此句的主干是 each review period shall not exceed 21 days。Unless otherwise 引导让步状语从句，意为"除非雇主要求中另有说明"。on which 引导定语从句，等于"when"，修饰 date，意为"雇主收到一份承包商文件和承包商通知的那个时候"。calculated from 过去分词短语作宾语补足语，意为"从……的日期算起"。

4. The design, the Contractor's Document, the execution and the completed Works shall comply with the country's technical standards, building, construction and environmental Laws, Laws applicable to the product being produced from the Works, and other standards specified in the Employer's Requirements, applicable to the Works, or defined by the applicable Laws.

设计、承包商文件、施工和竣工工程，均应符合工程所在国的技术标准、建筑、施工与环境方面的法律、适用于工程将生产的产品的法律以及雇主要求中提出的适用于工程或适用法律规定的其他标准。

句子中有多个主语和宾语，"the design""the Contractor's Document""the execution and the completed Works"是主语，shall comply with 是谓语，"the country's technical standards""building, construction and environmental Laws""Laws applicable to the product being produced from the Works"和"other standards"是宾语。其中"Laws applicable to the product being produced from the Works"中 applicable to 前省略了 which are，修饰 laws，意为"适用于工程将生产的产品的法律"。"Specified in the Employer's Requirements""applicable to the Works""or defined by the applicable Laws"是后置定语，修饰 other standards，意为"雇主要求中提出的适用于工程或适用法律规定的其他标准"。

Lesson 30 The Contractor

1. The Contractor's General Obligations

The Contractor shall design, execute and complete the Works in accordance with the Contract, and shall remedy any defects in the Works. When completed, the Works shall be fit for the purposes for which the Works are intended as defined in the Contract.

The Contractor shall provide the Plant and Contractor's Documents specified in the Contract, and all contractor's Personnel, Goods, consumables and other things and services, whether of a temporary or permanent nature, required in and for this design, execution, completion and remedying of defects.

The Works shall include any work which is necessary to satisfy the Employer's Requirements, or is implied by the Contract, and all works which (although not mentioned in the Contract) are necessary for stability or for the completion, or safe and proper operation, of the Works.

The Contractor shall be responsible for the adequacy, stability and safety of all Site operations, of all methods of construction and of all the Works.

The Contractor shall, whenever required by the Employer, submit details of the arrangements and methods which the Contractor proposes to adopt for the execution of the Works. No significant alteration to these arrangements and methods shall be made without this having previously been notified to the Employer.

2. Performance Security

The Contractor shall obtain (at his cost) a Performance Security for proper performance, in the amount and currencies stated in the Particular Conditions if an amount is not stated in the Particular Conditions, this Sub-Clause shall not apply.

The Contractor shall deliver the Performance Security to the Employer within 28 days after both Parties have signed the Contract Agreement. The Performance Security shall be issued by an entity and from within a country (or other jurisdiction) approved by the Employer, and shall be in the form annexed to the Particular Conditions or in another form approved by the Employer.

The Contractor shall ensure that the Performance Security is valid and enforceable until the Contractor has executed and completed the Works and remedied any defects. If the terms of the Performance Security specify its expiry date, and the Contractor has not become entitled to receive the Performance Certificate by the date 28 days prior to the expiry date, the Contractor shall extend the validity of the Performance Security until the Works have been completed and any defects have been remedied.

The Employer shall not make a claim under the Performance Security, except for amounts to which the Employer is entitled under the Contract in the event of:

(1) failure by the Contractor to extend the validity of the Performance Security as described in the preceding paragraph, in which event the Employer may claim the full amount of the Performance Security,

(2) failure by the Contractor to pay the Employer an amount due, as either agreed by the Contractor or determined under Sub-clause 2.5 [Employer's Claims] or Clause 20 [Claims, Disputes and Arbitration], within 42 days after this agreement or determination,

(3) failure by the Contractor to remedy a default within 42 days after receiving the Employer's notice requiring the default to be remedied, or

(4) circumstances which entitle the Employer to termination under Sub-Clause 15.2 [Termination by Employer], irrespective of whether notice of termination has been given.

The Employer shall indemnify and hold the Contractor harmless against and from all damages, losses and expenses (including legal fees and expenses) resulting from a claim under the Performance Security to the extent to which the Employer was not entitled to make the claim.

The Employer shall return the Performance Security to the Contractor within 21 days after the Contractor has become entitled to receive the Performance Certificate.

3. Contractor's Representative

The Contractor shall appoint the Contractor's Representative and shall give him all authority necessary to act on the Contractor's behalf under the Contract. Unless the Contractor's Representative is named in the Contract, the Contractor shall, prior to the Commencement Date, submit to the Employer for consent the name and particulars of the person the Contractor proposes to appoint as Contractor's Representative. If consent is withheld or subsequently revoked, or if the appointed person fails to act as Contractor's Representative, the Contractor shall similarly submit the name and particulars of another suitable person for such appointment.

The Contractor shall not, without the prior consent of the Employer, revoke the appointment of the Contractor's Representative or appoint a replacement. The Contractor's Representative shall, on behalf of the Contractor, receive instructions under Sub-Clause 3.4 [Instructions].

The Contractor's Representative may delegate any powers, functions and authority to any competent person, and may at any time revoke the delegation. Any delegation or revocation shall not take effect until the Employer has received prior notice signed by the Contractor's Representative, naming the person and specifying the powers, functions and authority being delegated or revoked.

The Contractor's Representative and all these persons shall be fluent in the language for communications defined in Sub-Clause 1.4 [Law and Language].

4. Subcontractors

The Contractor shall not subcontract the whole of the Works.

The Contractor shall be responsible for the acts or defaults of any Subcontractor, his agents or employees, as if they were the acts or defaults of the Contractor. Where specified in the Particular Conditions, the Contractor shall give the Employer not less than 28 days' notice of:

(1) the intended appointment of the Subcontractor, with detailed particulars which shall include his relevant experience,

(2) the intended commencement of the Subcontractor's work, and

(3) the intended commencement of the Subcontractor's work on the Site.

New Words and Expressions

1. valid/validity 有效的/有效期
2. enforceable 可执行的
3. termination 终止
4. instructions 指示
5. subcontract v. 分包
6. subcontractor 分包商
7. take effect 生效
8. performance security 履约担保

9. particular conditions 专用条件

10. expiry date 期满日期

11. be entitled to 有权

12. make a claim 提出索赔

13. remedy a default 纠正违约

14. pay the Employer an amount due 雇主应付金额

15. irrespective of 不管

16. indemnify and hold the Contractor harmless against and from all damages, losses and expenses 保障并保持承包商免受所有损害赔偿费、损失和开支的伤害。

17. performance certificate 履约证书

18. appoint the Contractor's Representative 任命承包商代表

19. give him all authority necessary to act on the Contractor's behalf under the Contract 授予他代表承包商根据合同采取行动所需要的全部权力

20. intended commencement date 拟开工日期

21. submit to the Employer for consent 提交给雇主，以取得同意

22. the name and particulars of the person the Contractor proposes to appoint as Contractor's Representative 拟任命为承包商代表的人员姓名和详细资料

23. if consent is withheld or subsequently revoked 如未获同意，或随后撤销同意

24. fails to act as Contractor's Representative 不能担任承包商代表

25. appoint a replacement 任命替代人员

26. delegate any powers, functions and authority to any competent person 可向任何胜任的人员付托任何职权、任务和权力

27. shall give the Employer not less than 28 days' notice of 应在不少于 28 天前向雇主通知以下事项

Notes

1. If the terms of the Performance Security specify its expiry date, and the Contractor has not become entitled to receive the Performance Certificate by the date 28 days prior to the expiry date, the Contractor shall extend the validity of the Performance Security until the Works have been completed and any defects have been remedied.

如果在履约担保的条款中规定了其期满日期，而承包商在该期满日期 28 天前尚无权拿到履约证书，承包商应将履约担保的有效期延至工程竣工和修补完任何缺陷

时为止。

此句的主干是 the Contractor shall extend the validity。句中的 if…prior to the expiry date 是整个句子的条件状语从句,并且是个并列句。前一分句主语是 terms,另一分句的主语是 Contractor。第二分句中 by the date 是介词短语作时间状语,28 days prior to the expiry date 修饰 date,意为"在该期满日期 28 天前"。until 引导时间状语从句,意为"有效期延至……为止。"

2. The Employer shall not make a claim under the Performance Security, except for amounts to which the Employer is entitled under the Contract in the event of:

(1) failure by the Contractor to extend the validity of the Performance Security as described in the preceding paragraph, in which event the Employer may claim the full amount of the Performance Security,

除出现以下情况雇主根据合同有权获得的金额外,雇主不应根据履约担保提出索赔:

(1) 承包商未能按前一段所述延长履约担保的有效期,这时雇主可以索赔履约担保的全部金额;

此句的主干是 The Employer shall not make a claim。except for amounts 对句子主干起到补充说明的作用,意为"除了……金额外,雇主不应提出索赔"。under the Performance Security 是介词短语作条件状语,修饰 make a claim,意为"根据履约担保提出索赔"。to which the Employer is entitled under the Contract in the event of 修饰 amounts,in the event of 相当于 when,是介词短语作条件状语,修饰 is entitled,under the Contractor 也修饰 is entitled,意为"出现以下情况时,根据合同有权获得的金额"。

failure by the Contractor to extend the validity of the Performance Security as described in the preceding paragraph 修饰 in the event of。to extend the validity of the Performance Security 修饰 failure,意为"未能延长履约担保的有效期"。句中 by the Contractor 修饰 failure,前面省略了 which is made。As described in the preceding paragraph,相当于 which is described,修饰 extend,意为"按前一段所述延长……"。in which event 指 failure to extend the validity 这种情况,相当于 when,作 the Employer may claim the full amount of the Performance Security 的时间状语,意为"这时(当承包商未能按前一段所述延长履约担保的有效期时)"。

3. The Employer shall indemnify and hold the Contractor harmless against and from all damages, losses and expenses (including legal fees and expenses) resulting from a claim under the Performance Security to the extent to which the Employer was not entitled to make the claim.

雇主应保障并保持承包商免受因雇主根据履约担保提出的超出雇主有权索赔范

围的索赔引起的所有损害赔偿费、损失和开支（包括法律费用和开支）的伤害。

此句的主干是 The Employer shall indemnify and hold the Contractor harmless against and from all damages, losses and expenses。indemnify and hold the Contractor harmless against and from,意为"保障并保持承包商免受……的伤害"。Resulting from a claim under the Performance Security 作定语,修饰 all damages, losses and expenses,意为"因……而引起的所有损害赔偿费、损失和开支"。to which 是其引导的定语从句中的程度状语,修饰 the Employer,意为:"超出雇主有权索赔范围",而 to the extent 引导定语从句,修饰 claim,under the Performance Security,也修饰 claim,意为"根据履约担保提出的,超出雇主有权索赔范围的索赔"。

4. Unless the Contractor's Representative is named in the Contract, the Contractor shall, prior to the Commencement Date, submit to the Employer for consent the name and particulars of the person the Contractor proposes to appoint as Contractor's Representative.

除非合同中已写明承包商代表的姓名,承包商应在开工日期前,将其拟任命为承包商代表的人员姓名和详细资料提交给雇主,以取得同意。

此句的主干是 the Contractor shall submit to the Employer the name and particulars of the person。Unless 引导让步状语从句,修饰整个句子,意为"除非合同中已写明承包商代表的姓名"。prior to 是时间状语,意为"在……之前"。for consent 作目的状语,修饰动词 submit,意为"以取得同意"。the Contractor proposes to appoint as Contractor's Representative 是 person 的后置定语,意为"承包商拟任命为承包商代表的人员"。

Translation for Reference

参 考 译 文

第一课 土木工程

土木工程是对被建造环境的规划、设计、建造以及管理。这里所说的被建造环境包括根据科学原理所建造的所有的结构物：小到灌溉系统和排水系统，大到火箭发射设备。

土木工程师们修建道路、桥梁、隧道、大坝、港口、电厂、供水和排污系统、医院、学院、公共交通以及其他对现代和密集人口生活很重要的公共设施。土木工程师们也修建飞机场、铁路、输油管道、摩天大厦和其他大型结构等民用设施，以供工业、商业或者居住使用。除此之外，土木工程师还规划、设计和建设完整地城市和城镇，而且最近已经在计划和设计太空站平台来安放独立的社区。

"civil"一词派生于拉丁语的"公民"一词。1782年，英国人约翰·斯密顿首次提出用"civil"这一术语来对他所做的非军事工程和当时占主导地位的军事工程加以区分。从那时起，土木工程师一词常常就是指那些建造公共设施的工程师，不过现在这个词的领域又宽得多了。

研究范围。由于土木工程学科的研究范围很广，因此又被进一步细分成许多技术专业。一个工程根据其类型的不同，可能需要很多不同专业技术的土木工程专家。当一个项目开始，土木工程师要对场地进行测绘，确定供水、排污及电力线管的位置。岩土工程专家通过土工试验确定地基土是否能承担建筑物的荷载，环境专家研究项目对当地的影响：潜在的空气和地下水污染，该项目对当地动物和植物的影响以及如何设计项目以满足政府旨在保护环境的需要。交通专家决定什么样的设施是必要的，以减轻当地公路和其他交通网络由于完成该项目而造成的负担。同时，结构专家使用初步数据，为该项目制定详细的设计、计划和说明书。从项目的开始到结束，监督和协调这些土木工程师的工作，都是施工管理专家实施的。根据其他专家提供的信息，施工管理土木工程师估算材料和劳动力的数量和成本，安排所有工作的进度，订购工作所需的材料和设备，雇佣承包商和分包商，并进行其他监督工作以确保项目按时按质完成。

在任何工程项目实施的过程中，土木工程师都要广泛利用计算机。计算机用来设计工程中各种各样的要素(计算机辅助设计，CAD)并且管理它们。计算机是现代土木工程师所必需的，因为它可以帮助工程师通过有效地处理大批量的数据来确定完成项目的最佳方案。

结构工程。这一专业中，土木工程师要计划和设计所有类型的结构，包括桥梁、大坝、电厂、设备支座、海岸工程的特殊结构、美国太空计划、发射塔、巨型天文射电望远镜及其他很多类的工程结构。结构工程师利用计算机确定结构必须承受的荷载，还要考虑它的自重、风和飓风荷载、温度变化，这些温度变化会引起相应的建筑材料，如钢材、混凝土、塑料、石材、沥青、砖、铝或者其他建材的膨胀和收缩。

水资源工程。这一专业的土木工程师要处理水的物理调节的各个方面。他们的研究领域包括防洪、城市供水和灌溉用水、管理和控制江河以及水资源流失，还包括维护海滩和其他滨水设施。此外，他们设计海港、运河和水闸并加以维护，建造包括大型水电站的水坝工程和小型水坝在内的各种各样的集水工程，帮助设计海上结构，并且确定影响航运的结构位置。

岩土工程。这一领域的土木工程专家分析研究支撑结构以及影响其变形行为的岩石和土的特性。他们要计算由于建筑物或其他结构物自重压力引起的沉降，并通过一定的方法使沉降最小化。岩土工程师还要评价斜坡及填土的稳定性并确定如何提高其稳定性的方法，以及确定如何保护结构不受地震作用和地下水影响的方法。

环境工程。在这个工程分支，土木工程师设计、建造并且监督饮用水安全供水系统以防止和控制供水的污染，既包括地表水也包括地下水。他们也设计、建造并且监督控制或消除土地和空气污染的工程项目。环境工程师还建造水厂和废水处理厂，设计空气净化器和其他设备来减少或消除由工业生产、焚化或者其他排烟行为引起的空气污染。他们也要通过建造特殊的堆场来控制有毒和危险的垃圾或对它们进行中和处理。另外环境工程师还要设计和管理卫生填埋场以防止污染周围土地。

运输工程。从事这一专业的土木工程师要修建保证人和货物安全有效运输的设施。他们专门研究设计和维护所有类型的运输设施，包括公路和街道、公共交通运输系统、铁路和飞机场进出口以及海港等。运输工程师在设计每项工程过程中除了应用科技知识以外，同时还要考虑经济、政治和各种社会因素。由于社区的质量直接与运输系统的质量有关，所以运输工程师要与城市规划者密切合作。

管道工程。在土木工程的这个分支中，工程师建造管道和相关设备，以运送液体、气体或固体，包括从煤浆(混合的煤和水)和半液体废料到水、油和各种非常易燃和不易燃的气体。管道工程师要做的工作还有：管道设计，评价管道对其所经过地区的经济和环境影响，选择管道材料——钢、混凝土、塑料或者多种材料相结合，并且掌握它们的安装技术、管道强度测试方法，并控制所运输材料的压力和流速。当运输危险材料时，安全也应当是主要的考虑因素。

建筑工程。在这个领域的土木工程师自始至终监督项目的建设。有时称他们为项目工程师。他们应用技术和管理技能,包括施工方法、计划、组织建筑项目实施,并且管理项目财务。他们要协调所有建筑活动的参与者:测量员,还有放样和修建临时施工通道的工人,开挖地基的工人,支模和浇筑混凝土的工人以及绑扎的工人。建筑工程师也要定期向业主报告施工进度。

小区和城市规划。从事这一土木工程分支的工程师要对城市内的小区或整个城市进行规划。这种规划要考虑的因素远比工程本身要考虑的多得多:在土地和自然资源开发利用过程中碰到的环境因素、社会和经济因素都是要考虑的关键因素。这一专业的土木工程师还要合理规划城市的一些必需设施,包括街道和公路、公共交通系统、飞机场、港口设备、城市供水和废水处理系统、公用建筑、公园和供娱乐的设施以及其他设施,以保证社会和经济发展与环境保护协调一致。

摄影测量学,测量学和绘图学。这一专业领域的土木工程师要精细测量地球表面以获得可靠数据为工程场地定位和设计服务。他们的工作经常要用到高科技方法,例如卫星和航空测量、摄像影像的计算机处理等。来自卫星的无线电信号,通过激光和声波束扫描,转换成地图,从而为隧道掘进、公路和大坝建设提供精确导向,使防汛潮和农田水利项目分布点的标图更加准确,对可能影响一项建筑工程或建筑物群使用的地下地质信息进行精确定位。

其他专业。工程管理和工程教育是两个附加的土木工程专业,它们不完全属于土木工程学科的范围,但是对这个学科是很必要的。

工程管理。很多土木工程师的职业最终转向了管理。与其他一开始就在管理工作岗位的人不同,土木工程师管理者把技术知识与组织协调劳动力、材料、机械设备和资金的能力结合起来。他们可以在市、县、州或者联邦政府工作;也可以在美国军队工程师的小组内作为军事或者民事管理工程师;或者在半自治地区或城市的当局或者类似组织工作。他们也可能管理规模从几个到数百雇员的私人工程公司。

工程教育。选择教育职业的土木工程师通常教工程专业,包括研究生和本科生两个层次。很多从事教育的土木工程师致力于基础研究工作,从而最终在建筑材料和建筑方法等方面取得技术革新。很多人也担任工程项目的顾问,或者担任和重大项目相关的技术委员会的顾问。

第二课　水利工程

水利工程是关于水资源利用和水控制工程的一个分支。它主要涉及自然水资源的合理使用,例如海洋、河流、湖泊和地下水的合理使用,以及借助水工结构防止水灾的发生,因此它也涉及水工结构的建造以及对这一过程的监理。

水利工程包括诸如水路运输、水力发电,水资源对土壤的改进、给水排水以及淡水资源的利用。在这些分支当中,不管是属于水资源利用还是属于防洪工程,都需要建造水工结构。例如,为了利用储存在水中的能量,通过建造大坝提高水位以获得必要的水位差来驱动水力进行发电。必须为航运企业建造航标、港口、闸门以及船舶制造和维修所需的特殊结构。航道和码头都需要疏浚来维持正常运作。在水资源保护项目中,灌溉、排水、防洪等各种特殊结构都需要建造。这些特殊结构都称为水工结构。

水利工程的这些不同方面能够被联合起来形成一个综合的项目。例如,一条河流能够进行船运、创造能源、水资源供给、灌溉以及发展渔业。建在河流上的水库能够缓减洪灾、有序灌溉、发电,与此同时,它也促进了船运和渔业的发展。

社会和经济因素在水利工程项目中也扮演着重要的角色,不同部门之间的利益有可能会产生冲突,全方位地去解决这些冲突,对于水利工程项目计划的正确实施是至关重要的。

水路运输

在所有的地面运输体系当中,水运几乎与地球上的人类聚居一样古老。人类最初开发资源就是使用水路的方式从一个地方运到另一个地方。这样就导致新大陆和新资源的发现,而体积庞大、设计良好、装备齐全的海洋通行船也随之产生了。水路必须有足够的深度以供船只顺利通过,不同的船只对水深有不同的要求,并且应当提供相应的航海标记。

在我国水路运输的潜力是巨大的,作为运输的河流总计大约有 100 000 km,除此之外,沿着海岸线还有大量的海湾和深水出水口。这些条件非常适合建造港口。因此,水治理和水资源保护在中国扮演着重要的角色。它与中国人的生活和工作紧密相关。

海港码头

码头是一个为船只提供庇护的场所并且具有这样的设施:能够方便上船和下船的客人休息,各种货物的装卸及储存,同时将各种交托进行分类,为船只提供综合的服务。它是一个运输中心,港口是一个码头的重要部分,港口是能够使船只不受风暴和海浪袭击的部分封闭的海域。在这里，有提供燃料、修理、货物处理以及其他服务设施。港口结构在水利工程中有着重要的作用，这将在本书的后面部分进行介绍。

水力发电

水力发电项目是一项规模最大、耗资最大和最引人注目的土木工程构筑物。我们只要想到尼亚加拉瀑布发电工程、阿斯旺高坝、沃尔特河或斯诺伊山等工程项目，就可以认识到这一点。更重要的是，水力发电站的施工经常与河流的综合利用联系在一起，因此对国民经济的发展有重要意义。阿旺斯高坝使埃及的可耕地面积增加30%以上，并且可以控制尼罗河的洪水灾害，并提供 50 万 kW 的电力。

一个典型的水力发电站是由一个水库、一个由钢筋混凝土建造的厂房、一个与室内的发电机相连的水涡轮以及其他的一些机械/电子设备组成的。一个水库对于维持水电站的平衡工况起着重要的作用。水库里储存的水能够为水涡轮提供所需的流速，以确保不被自然流速影响，进而也保证了用户所需要的电能。

灌溉

在农业方面，如果水对土壤的自然供给不充足，则需要人工供水进行作物灌溉来保证作物的正常生长。在许多情况下，这些水来自水库。通常水库中的水首先被用来发电，然后才用来灌溉。因此，一个灌溉系统包括水资源、取水结构、渠道、配送水的管道，与渠道网相联系的结构，排放过量水的渠道。

与灌溉系统设计相关的一些问题，例如，确定灌溉区域、水及水资源的数量、取水和灌溉的方法、灌溉系统的配送、结构的细部结构等必须依靠水利专家、农学专家及经济学家的合作而得以解决。

排水

排水涉及人工去除田地和土壤中过剩的水，这些过剩的水对庄稼是有害的并且很有可能形成沼泽。

排水技术包括：(1) 通过建造堤坝、挖渠道来阻止水进入进水闸；(2) 使用排水沟带走地表水和地下水。在城市及工业化地区，排水系统通常设在地下。

水土保持

土壤侵蚀是土壤被水和风冲刷的现象。一方面，土壤侵蚀移除了表面的肥沃土壤；另一方面，它增加了在河流中的沉积物，而这些沉积物可能充满河流甚至使河流荒芜。此外，水土流失使地面不能被雨水渗透，造成更频繁的洪水。为了避免这些灾难，应增加地面的渗透能力从而减少径流量和径流速度，提高土壤经受侵蚀的能力。这样的水和土壤的维护工作就是所谓的水土保持。

洪水控制

建造堤坝是为了阻止洪水，然而，在绝大多数的情况下仅有堤坝并不能最终解决问题。随着沉淀的不断进行,相应的河床逐步升高。因此,在现代的防洪控制中必须采取综合的措施。除了建造堤防设施外,在防洪控制中,还有两个主要的方面。一个就是增加河流的排水量,例如,通过疏浚河床达成此目的。另一个是在上游切断和储存洪水,例如在那里建造大坝以调节径流。需要强调的是水土保持是洪水控制的基本措施,因为如果水土完好的话,径流可大大减少。

供水工程

水供给应该在数量上足够在质量上优质。首先,应该估计水量,然后评价水资源、分析水质。一个供水系统包括三个部分:取水、水处理和水的分配。水资源对供水系统影响最大。

地表水,如河水,往往比较浑浊,包含大量的有机物质和细菌以及相对少量的矿物质,因此它主要用于工业。地下水通常适合作为饮用水供给系统的水源。

水处理的主要方法包括净化(沉淀、过滤)、消毒和软化。有时这个过程也包括除锈、蒸馏和空气消毒。

三峡工程概述

在过去的几百年里,水利工程已经取得了很大的发展,巨大的水力发电站,成千上万米长的运河,宏大的灌溉及排水项目已经被完成。中国的三峡工程是最著名的。

三峡工程的主体结构包括蓄水大坝、泄洪设施、发电站和导航设施。大坝是一个混凝土重力坝,最大高度175～180 m和总长2 500～2 800 m,泄洪道部分建立在河道的中间。在大坝底有两个发电站,导航设施设置在左岸。

第三课 测量与绘图

没有绘图,也可以说就没有土木工程。而土木工程师都必须知道绘图的元素以及如何获得绘图所需的测量结果,这一过程在英语中被称为测量。如果一块土地没有小山或许多建筑物就可以用钢尺准确测得,但是当这块土地有多于四条边或者它的边长超过1 000米时,用钢尺就很难测得了。一块很小的土地,有许多障碍物遮住视线时,使用钢尺是不能精确测量的,而这里则需要一个能够精确测量角度的仪器。测量中,用来测量角度的仪器就被称作经纬仪。

这些仪器可以提供画图时所需要的信息,但是若用水准测量仪则更加简单和准确。普通类型被称为定镜水准仪,它就像一个经纬仪一样被固定在一个三脚架上,以使得视线处在地面上的一个较方便的高度,由此测量者就可以轻松地找到测量点。许多三脚架是可伸缩的,它们的腿架长度可有很大的伸缩性。

所有土地的测量都基于一系列相关联的三角形。整个区域应该尽量被设定好的三角形覆盖。借助经纬仪,就可以根据三角形的已知夹角和已测边长得到未测边长。

还有三种测量仪器是应当提及的,它们是铅锤、平板仪和视距仪。

铅锤是一种上端用一根细绳吊在经纬仪下方的重体,用来保证仪器中心对准测量的站点。平板仪是处在三脚架上的画板,可以在不同的点。当长度和角度确定后绘图也就完成了。视距仪通常和平板仪一起使用。视距仪是一个普通的地球仪,只不过它配有望远镜的上下平行的视距丝。视距丝之间一米的距离就相当于实际一百米的距离。将视距尺放在需要测距的那个点上,记录上丝和下丝在该尺上的读数,就可以算出视距尺和仪器间的距离。测量的人读出该仪器测得的数据给他的助手,助手算出它们之间的距离乘以100,就可以得出这个点与仪器的距离。

随着科学技术的发展,更先进的测量设备随之问世。GPS(全球定位系统)就是其中的一个。它把全球定位技术与计算机、空间和现代通信技术紧密地结合在了一起。

第四课　钢筋混凝土

素混凝土是由水泥、水、细骨料、粗骨料(碎石或卵石)、空气,通常还有其他外加剂等经过凝固硬化而成。将可塑的混凝土拌和物注入模板内,并将其捣实,然后进行养护,以加速水泥与水的水化反应,最后获得硬化的混凝土。其最终制成品具有较高的抗压强度和较低的抗拉强度,其抗拉强度约为抗压强度的十分之一。因此,截面的受拉区必须配置抗拉钢筋和抗剪强度以增加钢筋混凝土构件中较弱的受拉区的强度。

由于钢筋混凝土截面在均质性上与标准的木材或钢的截面存在差异,因此,需要依据机构设计的基本原理进行修改。将钢筋混凝土这种非均质截面的两种组成部分按一定比例适当配置,可以优化其中材料的使用性能。这一要求是可以达到的,因混凝土由配料搅拌成湿拌和物,经过振捣并凝固硬化,可以做成任何一种需要的形状。如果拌制混凝土的各种材料配合比恰当,则混凝土制成品的强度较高,经久耐用,配置钢筋后,可以作为任何结构体系的主要构件。

浇筑混凝土所需的技术取决于即将浇筑的构件类型,诸如:柱、梁、墙、板、基础、大体积混凝土水坝或者继续延长已浇筑完毕并且已经凝固的混凝土等。对于梁、柱、墙等构件,当模板清理干净后应该在其上涂油,钢筋表面的锈及其他有害物质也应该被清除干净。浇筑基础前,应将坑底土夯实并用水浸湿大约 6 英寸的深度,以免土壤从新浇筑的混凝土中吸收水分。一般情况下,除使用混凝土泵浇筑外,混凝土都应在水平方向分层浇筑,并使用插入式或表面式高频电动振捣器捣实。必须记住,过分的振捣将导致骨料离析和混凝土泌浆等现象,因而是有害的。

水泥的水化作用发生在有水分存在、而且气温在 50°F 以上的条件下。为了保证水泥的水化作用得以进行,必须具备上述条件。如果干燥过快则会出现表面裂缝,这将有损于混凝土的强度,同时也会影响到水泥水化作用的充分进行。

设计钢筋混凝土构件时显然需要处理大量的参数,诸如宽度、高度等几何尺寸,配筋的面积,钢筋的应变和混凝土的应变,钢筋的应力等等。因此,在选择混凝土截面时需要进行试算并作调整,根据施工现场条件、混凝土原材料的供应情况、业主提供的特殊要求、对建筑和净空高度的要求、所用的设计规范以及建筑物周围环境条件等最后确定截面。钢筋混凝土通常是现场浇筑的合成材料,它与工厂中制造的标准的钢结构梁、柱等不同,因此对于上面所提供的一系列因素必须予以考虑。

在结构系统中的每个关键位置都要选择试算截面。试算截面必须经复核以确定其名义强度是否足以承受所施加的荷载。由于经常需要一个以上的试验到达需要试算的截面,第一个设计输入步骤是生成一系列的试验和调整分析。

选择混凝土截面时,采用试算与调整过程可以使复核与设计结合在一起。因此,当试算截面选定后,每次设计都是对截面进行复核。手册、图表和微型计算机以及专用程序的使用,使这种设计方法更为简捷有效,而传统的方法则是把钢筋混凝土的复核与单纯的设计分别地进行处理。

第五课　土的工程性质

对土的工程性质来说，决定用于工程使用的指标包括内摩擦、黏结力、压缩性、弹性、渗透性和毛细现象。

内摩擦是土体滑动所产生的抗滑现象。砂和砾石比黏土的内摩擦要大；在黏土中增加水分会降低内摩擦。在建筑物自重作用下土的滑动趋势以剪切的方式发生；也就是说，土体在平面上移动要么水平，要么垂直或是其他方式。这样的剪切移动对建筑物是危险的。

抗剪破坏也是土的黏结力的特性，它是土颗粒相互作用产生的，与土颗粒之间的分子力和水存在有关。黏结力明显受到水分的含量影响。对于干砂来说，黏结力是零，对非常硬的黏土黏结力可达到 100 kPa。

压缩性是土的一个重要特性，可以用滚动、夯实、震动或其他手段压实土壤，由此可增加它的密实度和承载能力。

任何有弹性的土在压实后会趋于恢复到原有状态。弹性土（膨胀土）作为柔性道路路基是不合适的，因为当车辆经过时会产生压实和膨胀，这样会引起道路破坏。

渗透性是允许水通过土渗流的一种性质。在冬天的冻融循环、夏天的湿干循环会改变土颗粒的密度。压实会使渗透性减小。

毛细作用可以通过高于自由水正常水平面的土壤使水升高。对大部分土来说有大量毛细作用通道存在。在黏土中由于毛细作用，水可以升高 30 英尺。

密度可以用重量与体积测量或用专用测量装置来确定。土的稳定性由稳定仪来测定，它可测定由垂直荷载引起的水平力。固结是指在特定荷载条件发生的土壤的挤密或压合。这种性质是可检验的。

第六课 工程地质学在不列颠哥伦比亚省的发展

导言

　　工程地质学是地质学的一个分支学科。工程地质学者把关于岩石、土壤和地下水的地质学原理应用于各类工程建筑的选址、设计和施工以及对各种自然和人为灾害的缓解措施进行评估设计。工程地质学者从事的工作与传统的地质工作者相距甚远,他们在研究中使用的方法也与传统地质工作者不同。

　　本文认为,工程地质学在不列颠哥伦比亚的发展大致可分为三个阶段。在 1920 年以前,在该省的工程项目中并未有意考虑地质学问题。在 1920 到 1945 年间,如果工程项目必须或要求提供地质信息,通常由传统地质工作者提供。1945 年以后,在该省,经专门训练的、富有经验的工程地质学者开始进行工程实践并参与到当时的工程项目之中。到 20 世纪 60 年代,在不列颠哥伦比亚,工程地质学已经比较完善并成为公认的地质学分支学科之一。

工程地质学在不列颠哥伦比亚

1920 到 1945 年

　　1921 年,不列颠哥伦比亚大学开始教授地质工程学,但它仅与采矿和石油地质相关,而与土木工程无关。在 1920 到 1945 年间,不列颠哥伦比亚开始发展,建设了一些大的工程项目。1919 年,当时公共工程部想要改善弗雷泽河三角洲的航运条件,加拿大地质勘探局的 W. A. 约翰逊完成了一次地质调查,用来确定在改善该河的适合航运部分时可以采用的工程方法。这可能是该省用于工程项目的首次地质调查。

　　维克托·多尔梅奇,加拿大地质勘探局的硬岩采矿地质学家,在 1922 到 1929 年间任不列颠哥伦比亚分局的局长,绘制了该省许多地区的基岩地质图。1927 年,他完成了米申山隧道的地质图,开始了他的工程地质事务。1929 年,他作为采矿地质学家开始从事私人顾问工作,并在不列颠哥伦比亚大学兼职教授地质工程课程。他的学生之一是后面将要提到的杰克·阿姆斯特朗博士。1930 年多尔梅奇为位于卡比兰诺河的克利夫兰大坝和用于大温哥华地区供水和排水工程的"第一海湾"压力隧道提供了地质咨询。维克托·多尔梅奇可以被看作是不列颠哥伦比亚的第一位工程地质学家,虽然他没有受过相关教育。

　　在这一时期对工程项目作出过贡献的地质学家还有 D. F. 基德和 H. C. 冈宁,他们都出自加拿大地质勘探局。基德离开勘探局后开始了自己的业务,而冈宁到不列颠哥伦比亚大学教书并在后来成为地质学系主任和应用科学学院院长。他们在工程地质学方面的工作价值与多尔梅奇相比是较小的。

1945 年到 1960 年

二战后初期是不列颠哥伦比亚的繁荣时期。在这一时期构思、设计和建造了大量的大坝、纸浆和造纸厂、隧道和大型工厂。其间，多尔梅奇仍作为采矿地质学咨询专家，参与了许多这类大项目，包括不列颠哥伦比亚电力公司的许多项目，诸如布里奇河电站、瓦里奇湖电力项目、切卡穆斯湖电力项目、约旦河项目以及 W.A.C. 本尼特大坝。他还参加了大部分用于向大温哥华地区供水和排水工程的温哥华地区的过水涵洞的工作，并对加拿大铝业公司的沿海岸大部分提议坝址进行了地质状况评估，其中包括 14.5 km 长的基马诺涵洞。

1955 年后多尔梅奇在名为多尔梅奇·梅森·斯图尔特的公司几乎专门从事工程地质工作。他的工作包括 1957 年加拿大公共工程部在西摩峡湾的流纹岩爆破，这是当时最大的非核爆破。关于这个项目的论文，发表在加拿大采矿和冶金学会会刊上，获得了伦纳德金奖。1950 年多尔梅奇在《不列颠哥伦比亚职业工程师》第一卷发表了题为"坝址的地质勘察"的论文。

在 1930 和 1940 年代，卡尔·太沙基是哈佛大学的实践土木工程教授。他教的唯一课程是工程地质学。1945 年他作为艾伯尼港、坝贝尔河、纳奈莫、克罗夫顿和卡斯尔加的纸浆和造纸厂相关的土力学问题评审顾问，被 H.A. 西蒙斯请到西海岸，开始是在华盛顿州，后来在不列颠哥伦比亚。

他对该省的工程地质学有所重大影响，在他 1963 逝世后，不列颠哥伦比亚水电公司把米申大坝重新命名为太沙基大坝。

在 20 世纪 50 年代早期，不列颠哥伦比亚矿业局是该省唯一的在员工中有地质专家的部门，但他们都是硬岩专家，他们的工作都是与采矿相关的项目。其他部门，包括高速公路、农业、水资源和公共工程部门，需要提供土木工程方面的意见。因此，休·内史密斯被雇用了，他从不列颠哥伦比亚大学获得地质工程学位，又从华盛顿大学获得工程地质研究生学位。他是第一个在该省工作并为该省工作的受过专门训练的工程地质专家。他参与了从 20 世纪 50 年代早期到 1958 年的许多工程项目，1958 年他离开政府部门，到 R.C. 瑟伯及其合伙人公司，即现在的瑟伯工程有限公司，在那里继续参与工程项目。

与此同时，其他地质专家和工程地质专家也进入了这一领域。在 20 世纪 40 年代晚期，杰克·阿姆斯特朗，受过专门训练的硬岩地质专家、开始绘制温哥华和弗雷泽低地的地表地质图，此事促成了加拿大地质勘察文件《不列颠哥伦比亚弗雷泽低地的地表地质的环境和工程应用》出炉。

道格·坎贝尔，另一个接受经典地质学训练的地质专家，由多尔梅奇介绍进入工程地质领域。在 20 世纪 40 年代晚期，他参与了 W.A.C. 本尼特大坝的地质调查。同样也是在这一时期，工程地质专家杰克·莫拉德，在一个不列颠哥伦比亚电力公司的项目中,把航拍相片判读引入该省的工程地质领域。

1959年,在亨利·冈宁的推动下,不列颠哥伦比亚大学在地质工程专业开设了工程地质课程。

1960年至今

该省的持续发展在近些年带来了许多具有挑战性的大型工程项目。这对工程地质有持续的需求。受过良好训练的、经验丰富的工程地质工作者的数量有了增加,其中一些是全世界最优秀的。今天,工程地质在省政府许多部门、联邦政府机构、铁路和顾问公司中得到应用。虽然工程地质学对不列颠哥伦比亚的基岩地质图的绘制没多大影响,但它促进了地表地质学、地形学、地质活动、地下水和环境工作的研究。今天,形形色色的项目中都包含了工程地质工作者的工作,其中大坝是主要领域之一,因为工程地质工作者了解大坝建于何处更合适。

第七课　内陆航道

在内陆航道上航行是最古老的大陆运输方式。虽然在其悠久的发展史中，它已经经历了许多技术发展阶段并（在一些国家里）从繁荣走向衰退，但不可否认的是它构建了世界上许多国家运输基础设施中重要和不可缺少的一部分。

在古代文明中，内河航行在世界主要大河（尼罗河，幼发拉底河，恒河等）的河谷地带蓬勃发展，并且在古埃及，美索不达米亚都存在众所周知的人工开凿出的河道，还有中国的炀帝（公元611年隋朝）修建的"大运河"，一条2 400公里的水路（将北部的河流系统与南部的省份连接起来）。

在公元793年的欧洲，查理大帝试图开凿一条运河，旨在连接莱茵河和多瑙河（福萨卡罗莱纳州），但这个企图很快被放弃。第一个有明确记载的通航船闸可以追溯到1439年，被设置在意大利北部的Grand大运河上。

工业化是18世纪和19世纪现代水道发展的原动力，在英格兰建造的可通航的河沙运河网处于这种产业发展的最前沿（例如由詹姆斯·布林德利建造的布里奇沃特运河和由托马斯·特尔福德建造的埃尔斯米尔运河）。苏格兰的福斯和克莱德运河于1790年完工，是世界上第一个海边运河。

建于1875年的安德顿升船机，克服了特伦特—墨西运河与英国柴郡的韦弗河之间15米的高差，是第一台带有液压升降系统的铁驳升船机。

19世纪下半叶和20世纪初见证了两个具有全球重要性的通航运河的建成。其中160公里长、305～365米宽和19.5米（最小）深的苏伊士运河于1869年开通，缩短了欧洲和远东之间16 000公里的海上航线；现在每年被15 000艘船使用，包括150 000吨的油轮。长达80公里的巴拿马运河于1914年开通，连接大西洋和太平洋的运河长13公里，宽153米，穿过大陆分水岭和一个大型人工湖，并在入口和出口处设立了三个水闸，总抬升高度为26米。

目前欧洲的主体内陆航道网络是建立在现代化和扩充19世纪航运设施的基础之上的。这同样适用于美国主要航道的航运设施发展，例如密西西比河和俄亥俄河。虽然在20世纪内陆航道往往不能与铁路和后来的高速公路网竞争，但是他们保持甚至提升了在提供高效运输上的地位，特别是在散装材料的运输方面。

内陆航运在水资源管理方面、在提供现代娱乐设施运输方面以及在加强环境方面的作用进一步巩固了这种新的认识。

尽管其他运输方式在迅猛发展，但采用内陆航运运输有一些普遍适用的优点（Čábelka和Gabriel，1985年）：

(1) 能源需求低（内陆航行的具体能源消耗约为铁路的80%，小于公路运输消耗

的 30%);

(2) 单位运输产出的劳动生产率高;

(3) 单位运输量的材料需求低(铁路和公路运输的对应值分别为两倍和四倍高);

(4) 对环境的影响最低(低噪音,低排气量);

(5) 对土地的需求最低(在有可航行的河流的情况下);

(6) 与其他运输模式相比,事故发生率低;

(7) 能够轻松运输散装货物和大型工业产品。

关于内陆航运运输模型以及相关水力结构的设计和操作的详细的探讨,将会建立在假设读者熟知明渠流定义和公式或者至少有一些河流工程工作经验的基础之上。

第八课　内陆航道运输在中国的发展

中国的内河航道系统包括 5 600 多条可通航河流，通航总长度达到 119 000 km，是区域界别分组中最发达的内陆航道运输。全国的总内河通航里程多数集中在长江、珠江、淮河和黑龙江的航道上。仅长江（含支流）一条河道就含有通航里程 5 800 km，占全国总量的 50%，其中 3 000 km 航道可通行载重吨位为 1 000 及以上的船舶。除了这些主要的河流，还有一条古老的京杭大运河，目前通航里程达 1 747 km，但通航里程会随着航道治理工程而逐年加长。

在内河航道网中存在大约 2 000 个内陆港口，包括 85 个大型港口装备有 52 个可以停靠载重为万吨的船舶的码头，这其中的 7 个港口，每个都至少达到上千万吨的年货物吞吐量。航道网中还包括大约 900 个航道建筑物，例如船闸和升船机。其中最著名的是长江三峡大坝的五级船闸。

中国集中推动 5 个特定地区的内河航道发展，分别是长江、珠江、京杭大运河、长江三角洲和珠江三角洲。在湖南省的开发提案中，有 1 亿美元的世界银行贷款直接用于投资 2.2 亿美元的项目，期望此项目能带动一个拥有 600 万贫困人口的地区的繁荣。这笔贷款中的一大部分资金是提供给发电用水坝建设、绕行的船闸系统建设和整体航道的加深工程，以便利大型船只通航贸易。

其间在长江（带动全国 80% 的内河航道交通）流域，上海周边进行着巨大的商业和基础设施发展，上游的三峡大坝（尤其能改善电力输送）将会彻底改变坝上和坝下的船只通行规模以及货物和人口的移动条件。这项工程包括了世界上最大的船闸。这个船闸是双线五级船闸。单个闸室长 280 米、净宽 34 米、深 5 米，允许载重万吨的船队通过。船闸全长 1 607 米。当坝前正常蓄水位为海拔 175 米时，船闸上下落差可达 113 米，总投资基金为 7.47 亿美元。经过几年的建设，船闸于 2003 年 7 月 16 日正式通航。

第九课 河床演变

河床演变包括泥沙运动和对河床的冲刷和淤积作用。

流水的冲刷作用有两种方式。首先,穿过河床的水流直接对河床施加了一个剪应力。如果基底的黏结强度小于所施加的剪应力,或者河床由能被这种剪应力推动的松散的泥沙组成,那么河床将在清水作用下持续下降。然而,如果河流携带大量的泥沙,这些泥沙就可以作为增强河床的平滑度的工具(磨平)。同时,泥沙颗粒被碾碎,变得更小和更圆润。

河流中的泥沙作为推移质(在河床附近移动的粗糙颗粒碎片)或悬移质(在水中携带的较细颗粒碎片)被运输。还有一部分携带可溶解材料。

对于每个不同尺寸的颗粒,都存在使该颗粒开始运动的特定流速,称为启动速度。然而,由于启动后的颗粒和河床之间摩擦力的减少(或脱离),即使流速降低到启动速度以下,颗粒仍继续被带动。最终,速度将降到足够低才能使颗粒沉积。这种现象可以由 Hjulström 曲线来表示(如图 9-1)。

一条河在其河流全线,持续不断地带走和遗落流经河床上的岩石颗粒和土壤颗粒。在河流流动快的地方,拾起的颗粒比落下的多。在河流流动缓慢的地方,掉落的颗粒比拾起的多。掉落颗粒更多的区域称为冲积平原或洪泛平原,掉落的颗粒被称为冲积层。

大河的携沙量是巨大的。许多河流的名字源于携带物在水中的颜色。例如,黄河在中国根据字面意思被翻译成"黄色的河",美国的密西西比河也被称为"大泥河"。据估计,密西西比河每年向海上运送泥沙可达 4.6 亿吨,黄河为 7.96 亿吨,意大利的波河为 6 700 万吨。

第十课　通航运河

通航运河可以用于绕过难以航行的河段,并且可以用来连接单个拦河坝或者是连接与河道渠化工程中拦河坝的间距相比间隔较远的多个坝体。除此之外,它们是内陆航行中的关键部分,它们连接两个流域。它们需要形状合适的进口,一般是一个独立的流量调节建筑物和船闸。

在交通和地质的限制下,运河的位置和布局可以被调整用于适应一般运输、土地利用和工业需求。运河通常明显短于渠化河道,结合低(或零)流速,有助于在两个方向上的通航。它们的主要缺点是占用土地和断流。因此在规划运河时,只要开凿运河是可行的,应尽可能利用现有河流。

通航运河可在一个方向上有水位落差,或者当存在高位水库时两个方向上都有水位落差。为方便进出某个工业中心,它们可以连接两个河流系统或者成为某航道的分支。通航河流与运河的交汇处,由天然河流引出的运河分支或者分支运河可能会产生特殊的交通和施工问题。

临时或永久位于周边地下水水位之上的运河河段需要(除防腐蚀保护外)一些防止渗漏损失的保护手段;适当的地下排水和使用防渗或抗渗层(例如黏土、混凝土、塑料等)用于抵抗地下水位增加所产生的回压是必不可少的。渠化河道的护岸和运河的护岸是同类工程,随所在河流的类型不同而产生变化。

运河要有足够的深度和宽度,正如在常规的河流上,拖带船队要通过弯道,就需要弯道有更大的宽度。双线航道直线段航道最小宽度 B 为 $B = 3b$ 或 $B = 2b + \Delta b$,式中 b 为驳船(或一组驳船)的宽度,Δb 为侧间隙,$\Delta b \geqslant 5$ m。如果是单线航道,$B = (1.5 \sim 2)b$。

航道的最小弯曲半径 r 由典型驳船的长度 L 乘以某一常数取得,如为顶推船队,常数取 3 左右;如为拖带船队,常数取 4.5。双线航道弯曲段水道宽度必须被加宽为 $B_0 = B + \Delta B$ [图 10-1(a)],式中

$$\Delta B = \frac{L^2}{2r+B} \simeq \frac{L^2}{2r} \tag{10.1}$$

航道(偏转)转向角 α,是拖带船中心线与航道弯曲半径切线相交形成的夹角 [图 10-1(b)]。转向取决于弯道的半径,拖带船(拖船)的航速、马力和尺寸,拖带船的载重,风速和水流状况。拖带船队向下游方向航行产生的航道转向角比向上游方向航行时大。

美国陆军工程兵团(1980)依据德国长达 180 米拖带船在莱茵河航道的转向角数据,推断出:向下游航行,弯道半径 400 m<r<2 500 m 时,航道转向角 2°<α<15°。如

向上游航行,则转向角 α 的值减半。

根据美国陆军工程兵团得出的结论,以下公式适用于计算航道转弯段宽度 B_0:

单向航道,

$$B_{01} = L_1 \sin\alpha_d + b_1 + 2c \tag{10.2}$$

双向航道,

$$B_{02} = L_1 \sin\alpha_d + b_1 + L_2 \sin\alpha_u + b_2 + 2c + c' \tag{10.3}$$

式中 L 是拖带船的长度,为最大转向角,b 是拖带船的宽度,c 是拖带船和航道护岸间的空隙,c' 是双向拖带船队之间的空袭;后缀"d"表示下行,"u"表示上行拖带船。使用公式(10.3)得出的计算结果可以用公式(10.1)来校核。

第十一课　坝

据可靠记载,世界上第一座坝是公元前4000年以前在尼罗河上修建的。它使尼罗河改道,并为古老的孟菲斯城提供城址。至今仍在使用的最古老的坝是16世纪修建的西班牙阿尔曼扎坝。随着岁月的流逝,各种建筑材料和施工方法得到了改善,修建诺拉克这样的大坝才成为可能。该坝正在前苏联境内靠近阿富汗边界的瓦赫什河上施工,是一座高达1 017英尺(333米)的土石坝。大坝失事可能造成生命财产的严重损失。因此,坝的设计和维修通常是在政府监督下进行的。美国有3万多座坝由各州政府控制着。1972年(美国)联邦大坝安全法(PL92-367)规定,必须由合格的专家对大坝进行定期检查。在1976年6月爱达荷州提堂大坝失事后,美国对大坝安全更为关切。

1. 坝的类型

坝按其形式和建筑材料分为:重力坝、拱坝、支墩坝和土坝。前三种坝通常是用混凝土浇筑的。重力坝依靠自重维持稳定,通常在平面上呈直线状,不过有时也略带弧形。拱坝通过拱的作用把水的水平推力中的大部分传给地基,因此它的横截面比重力坝单薄些。拱坝只用于崖壁能承受拱作用所产生的推力的峡谷中。各种支墩坝中最简单的是平板坝,它是由许多支墩间隔地支撑着倾斜的面板。土坝是一种由土或石料填筑而成并借助于不透水的心墙或上游铺盖防渗透的土堤。在一座大坝的结构中可包含不止一种坝型。弧形坝可以把重力作用和拱作用结合起来,以利坝的稳定。长坝常常有一个包括溢洪道、泄水闸在内的混凝土坝段,其余坝段是用土或石填筑的副坝。

对于既定的坝址选择最佳坝型是一个关系到工程可行性及其造价的问题。工程可行性受地形、地质及气候条件所支配。例如:由于混凝土遭受冻融作用的交替影响而引起剥落,因此在低温地区常避免采用断面单薄的混凝土拱坝或支墩坝。各类坝的造价主要取决于能否在工地附近取得建筑材料和各种运输工具能否进入。大坝有时分期建造,第二期或以后各期工程,往往在第一期以后需要10年或更长的时间。

坝高定义为路面或溢洪道顶与基坑最低点之间的高程差。不过,引用的坝高值常常是用另外的一些方法确定的,往往取原河床以上的净高度作为坝高。

2. 作用在坝上的力

坝必须是相对不透水的,并能经受得住作用在这上面的各种力。这些作用力中最重要的是重力(坝体重量)、静水压力、扬压力、冰压力及地震力。这些力传给坝基和坝座,而坝基和坝座则对坝体产生一个大小相等方向相反的基础反力。某些特殊情况下还要考虑水库中沉积泥沙引起的静水压力的影响以及坝顶溢流所产生的动力作用。

坝的自重是其体积和材料比重的乘积。该力的作用线通过横剖面的形心。静水压力可同时作用在坝的上游面和下游面。静水压力的水平分力 H_h 是作用在坝面垂直投影上的力,对于单位宽度坝体而言其值为:

$$H_h = rh^2/2 \tag{11.1}$$

式中:r 为水的比重;h 是水深;该力的作用线在坝基以上 $h/3$ 处。静水压力的竖直分力等于坝面正上方的水重,并通过该水体的重心。

于压力作用下的水必然要在坝和坝基之间流动,因而产生了扬压力。扬压力的大小取决于基础的特性和施工方法。经常假定扬压力从上游面(坝踵)处的全部静水压力直线变化到下游面(坝趾)处的全部尾水压力。根据这一假设,扬压力 U 为:

$$U = r(h_1 + h_2)t/2 \tag{11.2}$$

式中:t 是坝基的宽度;h_1 和 h_2 分别是坝踵和坝趾处的水深。扬压力的作用线通过压力梯形的形心(图 11-1)。

一些坝的实测资料表明(图 11-2):扬压力比公式 11.2 所给出的值小得多。对扬压力的分布有各种不同的假设,美国垦务局认为重力坝的扬压力成直线变化,在坝踵处为全部扬压力的 2/3,到坝趾处为零。坝踵附近通常设有排水装置,以便排除渗流水量,减小扬压力。

第十二课　堰和溢洪道的设计

1. 定义：大坝和堰

大坝和堰都是建在河流断面上用于蓄水的水工建筑物。

大坝被定义为在山谷断面上建造的、用来为上游水库蓄水的大型建筑物。所有流量包括最大可能洪峰流量都必须受到设计的溢流道的限制。上游水位不能漫过坝顶。漫坝确实能导致坝体侵蚀还可能导致溃坝。

常规的堰是设计用来提高上游水位的：例如，用于给分水渠输水。小流量由溢洪道泄水槽限制出流。大流量可全线漫过堰顶。在堰的下游端，急流产生的动能在消能结构中被消除[图 12.1(a)和 12.2(a)]。

另一种类型的堰是最小能量损失(MEL)堰[图 12.1(b)和 12.2(b)]。MEL 堰是设计用来最小化溢流的总水头损失的，由此产生(理想状态)零流入。MEL 堰适用于平坦区域和近河口。

实际上，小型坝和常规堰之间的差异很小，并且术语中的"堰"或"小坝"经常通用。

2. 溢洪道

暴雨期间，大量的水流入水库，水库水位有可能升到坝顶以上。溢洪道这类建筑物是设计用来在可控(即安全)条件下"溢出"洪水。这样洪水可以在坝的下方(例如涵洞和底部出口)、坝体中(例如岩石坝)或坝的上方(即溢洪道)泄流。

大多数小型坝配备有溢洪结构(称为溢洪道)(如图 12.3)。溢洪道通常包括三个部分：堰顶、泄水槽和在下游端的消能设施。堰顶的设计要使溢洪道的泄流能力达到最大。泄水槽的设计要使洪水从坝上方(或避开坝体)流过(即输流)。消能设施的设计是用来消散(即"分解")水流在泄水槽下游底端产生的动能[图 12.1(a)和 12.2]。

有一种型式类似溢洪道的建筑物叫落差建筑物。由于其水力特性与标准溢洪道有着显著不同，因此将在另一章中介绍。

3. 讨论

虽然溢洪道是针对特定条件(设计条件：Q_{des} and H_{des})设计的，但是它必须能在一定流量范围内安全且高效地运行。

设计工程师通常根据设计流量选择最优的溢洪道外形。然后用一定范围的工作流量(例如从 $0.1\ Q_{des}$ 到 Q_{des})和紧急情况(即 $Q > Q_{des}$)下的流量验证溢洪道是否安全运行。

在下面的章节中，我们首先介绍堰顶计算，然后是泄水槽计算，接着是消能设施计算。最后描述完整的设计过程。

第十三课 泥沙运输

泥沙由水流携带从一个地方被运输到另一个地方。基于泥沙颗粒的尺寸和黏结程度以及水流的强度,输沙量大致与流速成正比或者说与流速的平方或立方值成正比。因此,加倍的流速可挟动多达八倍的泥沙量。在某些情况下,在一次暴雨事件中的输沙量比一年中的所有其他时间相加更多。

上述的比例效应,也能导致大量泥沙沉积。如果水道的某一横截面积由于加深或加宽而突然增大,例如,当水位高过河岸漫滩时,流速下降的同时挟沙能力以更快的速度降低,因此泥沙将易于沉积。这种现象是导致航道和港口中浅滩形成的常见原因,并且有时被用于促使泥沙沉淀在特定位置上,例如沉积阱。

船只航行能通过以下方式使河床和河岸的泥沙悬浮:
(1) 当水从船首移至船尾时,在船下和船周围的流动;
(2) 船只下方的压力波动;
(3) 螺旋桨气流撞击河床;
(4) 船首和船尾波浪搅动河床和破坏河岸。

图 13-1 图示出了船只航行而造成的表面泥沙缕流。

由船只航运引起的悬浮的泥沙可以迅速沉积(如果泥沙由砂砾大小的物质组成)或者保持悬浮状态(如果泥沙由非常细的粉砂或黏土颗粒大小的物质组成)。细小的泥沙悬浮体具有比水更大的密度,因此离开悬浮点后可将它视为异重流。后者推动泥沙从水路中心线移动到相对安静的停泊区,并在那里沉积。这种现象在几个地方已被记录了下来(例如,Kelderman 等人,1998)。

旋涡流是指水流绕过障碍物或诸如港口水池的开口处时形成的旋涡,具有复杂的三维圆形结构,底部向心流动而表面向外流动,中间形成相对静止的区域。在旋涡流附近经过的泥沙被吸入旋涡并被推向中心,在那里慢慢沉积,就像在搅拌杯中散开的茶叶。这种现象是船台、侧槽和停泊区泥沙淤积的常见原因。

天然河流的特征取决于其蜿蜒曲折和不断迁移的趋势,几何形状的无规律性和变化性,不断变化的水位和流量以及不同河床、河岸的组合带来的差异性。在开发和改进天然河流中遇到的许多问题都与航道线位以及泥沙入流过程和在水流中的运动形式有关。河床和河岸的冲刷和关键区域的淤积都能影响航道的深度、宽度和中心线位置,以及通航建筑物的操作和使用,如船闸,港口,泊船区和其他设施,如水力发电厂、污水系统和进水口。泥沙运动也可以影响河道的泄洪能力。

第十四课　航道整治结构

1. 一般原则

对于航道作业,很明显,设计者可使用的技术和方法有很多种。应该意识到,河道的开发和控制取决于特定项目的最终预期目标。因此,众多可选择的堤岸和护岸的尺寸和形状中,能否选出对特定河流状况最有效的解决方案在很大程度上取决于设计者的学历,阅历和经验。全部的供选方案不一定适用于所有情况,应根据河流的现场环境和大小做相应的调整。一些技术更适合于大型内陆航道,例如密西西比河水系,而同样技术就有可能不适合较小的内陆航道,例如路易斯安那州的红河。

有两种类型的航道整治建筑物:堤防和护岸。堤防,顾名思义,指利用并设法使河流的能量有利于河道系统,例如改进航道。护岸用于维持系统的现状,例如以减轻岸堤侵蚀。

2. 堤防

堤防通常是布置在河流弯道内侧的一系列堤坝,那里常有泥沙淤积。堤坝的功能在低水位时期会一直保持,但在高水位被漫过的时候堤坝的作用将被削弱或"抹去"。堤坝的主要功能有:(1)将河流的能量集中到单一河道中,以控制航道的位置和增加航道的深度;(2)影响河流的侵蚀和沉积特征,以改造航道的尺寸。多年来,堤坝有很多广为人知的名字,例如交叉拱(或防波堤),横向堤,十字堤,丁堤,十字坝,翼坝和丁坝。图 14-1 中展示了目前最常用的堤坝。

某些类型的控制工作在航道建设的早期阶段至关重要,而其他类型的控制工作主要用在项目的最终完善阶段。例如,在密苏里河航道的早期设计中,从未考虑使用水下基石。项目中添加这种基石用来提供额外的航道限制以实现最终目标,同时不要反过来限制住航道对高流量的输送能力。

在美国早期的内陆航道初始设计中,从来不考虑在第十章介绍的所谓环保修正。在认识到环保在河道整治工程中的重要价值之前,绝大部分美国的内陆航道系统已经被设计和建造完成了。事实上,由于设计重点的改变,随着时间的推移环保修订也在逐步实施。因此,修缮一些治导工程,例如堤坝,在改善环境的同时保留其缩窄内陆航道和减少维护性疏浚的初衷。

3. 护岸

护岸建筑物主要用于防止河流弯道外侧的堤岸侵蚀和河流改道,同时建成或保持理想的航道中心线。护岸措施通常由岩石制成,但在密西西比河下游,ACMs 已被有效地使用。图 14-2 展示了一个典型的岩石护坡。

第十五课 波 浪

港口波浪运动

对于任何港口在施工中和完工后，波浪运动都是很重要的。波浪力则对船只的操纵、结构的设计、下锚和停泊非常重要。波浪状况对航行航道的设计有显著的影响，因为波浪会影响航道的设计深度和宽度。

外海港口需要防护措施避免波浪的作用。由于短波和长波特性的不同，在设计中两种波浪对港口作用的考虑当然也是不同的。对于短波，港口的容许波浪运动问题是容易解决的。容许波高随船只尺寸的增大而增大。这个临界限制对于横浪取最小值，顶头浪取最大值。30 000 吨以下的船停泊的港口内波高不应高于 1 m。30 000 吨以上的船停泊的港口内船舶横摇和首摇的幅度不应超过 0.5 m。各种研究已经证实港内的长波总是与短波联合出现的。除非关闭口门，否则想要阻止长波(≥30 秒)透过防波堤传入港内是不可能的。长波运动问题往往比短波问题更难处理。长波对港池的不良影响有时可以通过规避能引起共振的自然环境和港池的几何形状而在一定程度上减少。

无论主体是短波还是长波，共振问题都是非常重要的。10～20 秒的风浪或涌浪可能在尺度较短的港池内引起共振效应，例如在入口和出口处都有自由振荡的港池内，当周期 T 等于 $4L\sqrt{gh}$，或者在半封闭口门的港池内周期 T 等于 $2L\sqrt{gh}$ 的情况下，都会引起港池的共振现象。其中 L 为港池长度，h 为港池水深，$\sqrt{gh}$ 是推进波的传播速度。这种现象在挪威的小峡湾和一些长方形的港池内频繁出现。

波玫瑰图

港口的规划和布置、海岸结构物的设计、施工和维护需要对波浪的相关知识有全面的了解。

在港口规划阶段，通常需要估算当地的波浪情况并得出波高和波向的统计数据。这些数据可以依据波玫瑰图(图 15-1)分析得到。通常情况下，获得分析所需的基本信息是非常困难的。在理想情况下，在特定位置的野外数据应该是已知的。要涵盖各种海况发生的情况，则需要最少 2～3 年连续的仪器观测数据。

破碎带

当波浪到达水深较浅的海滩时，它们将发生破碎。有三种类型的破碎波：崩破波、卷破波和激散波。崩破波容易出现在波陡较大的坡度较小的海滩。最危险的破碎波是卷破波，它发生在波峰传播速度比整个波形传播速度快的时候，波浪的前端开始下降，最后发展成一股射流，携夹着空气向波浪底部撞击，飞溅的浪花在卷破发生之前通常会抬升至波峰的高度。由于破碎波及其生成的沿岸流的存在,悬移质通常是在波浪破碎带进行输移。破碎带由海岸向深海一侧延伸至波浪破碎的位置。当我们对航道、港池及海岸结构物进行研究时,了解破碎带是非常重要的。

第十六课 港口水深

水深是港口设计中一个重要的技术特性,应该满足船舶的安全驾驶和系泊。通常来讲,港内船的龙骨以下的水深越大,船舶航行就越方便而且越安全。但是水深过大会增加港口的施工和维护成本。因此应该有一个能够让船安全航行而又不会产生太多额外费用的合适的水深。这就意味着应该定义一个恰当的富余深度。

富余水深的组成及确定

当设计水深时,有两种需要考虑的情况:
(a) 当起帆或者停泊时使船不致搁浅的最小富余水深;
(b) 减少船的操纵难度所需的富余深度。

对于前一种情况来说,导致船舶搁浅的因素可能包括:(1) 测深误差;(2) 船舶运动增加的额外吃水。而后者应考虑两方面的因素:一方面是船舶操纵对于富余深度的要求,另一方面是为保护主要引擎冷凝器不堵塞而需要的富余深度。上述要求的说明如图 16-1 所示。

水下测深误差及障碍物

水位变化。实际水位与测量值之间存在差异,这个差异可能来自于潮位测量误差或者预计误差。水位的预计误差通常是 0.2 米,然而,以每个港口验潮站的潮汐观测资料为基础,这种误差不会超过 0.01~0.02 米。

图表测量误差。港口工程测量规范给出水深 10 米以内时图的容许误差为 0.15 米;水深 20 米以内时容许误差为 0.2 米,水深超过 20 米时,容许误差是水深的五十分之一。

船舶抛锚所需富余量。当航行中的船舶需要紧急停泊时,它总是将两侧的锚向后方同时放下从而使船能够完全停止。就这一点而言,锚其实成为了航道上的障碍,出于这个考虑应该在龙骨以下设置足够的富余深度以避免锚碰到船底。锚从底部突出的尺寸取决于锚的型号、重量、尺寸和海床材料特性等(例如,100 000 吨船舶的锚重约 13 吨,紧急停泊时将从海底突出 1.3 米)。

第十七课　港口位置的选择

建港位置的选择取决于拟建地区的一些物理特征,例如深度、可用陆域面积、是否容易进入港口、是否可以保护港口免受波浪作用、水流作用以及泥沙。港口开发、未来维护和疏浚的初始投资成本可能在很大程度上取决于拟建港口位置的物理特性。本节将给出港口规划者在选择港口位置时必须要考虑到的一些主要物理特性。

基本物理指标

对于任何位置来说要想作为一个很好的候选港址,一个先决条件是,它应该位于一个受保护的区域,在一个岛屿后面,在一个深的自然湾内,或在一个受庇护的泻湖或河口内。

给定的场地条件不仅会影响如前所述的投资和维护成本,也是船舶安全运行的必要条件。下面的场地环境条件可能对船舶操作施加一些限制:

(1) 天文潮和风;

(2) 水位变化(风暴增水和风暴减水);

(3) 波浪(方向、振幅、高度);

(4) 海流;

(5) 雾和冰。

前面提到的场地条件的统计调查是必要的,用以估计各种条件下的最高水位以及其出现的频率和历时。利用这些信息,港口规划者可以评价出各个待选港址给出的"实施极限"。上述环境条件对船舶的影响应从停靠时船舶操纵和运营的角度同时考虑。

总体发展要求

如前所述,大多数第三代港口将成功归于自由贸易的作用,不仅能吸引跨国企业进入港区,增加商业运输量,发展他们的业务,而且可以提供大量的货物。因此港口选址应便于自由贸易政策的执行与管理,也就是说我们最好将港址、保税区、出口和进口贸易区进行同步规划。

港址选择应吸引工业场区的建立,为促进城市和区域的经济发展提供更多的机会。

除了客运港,其他港的港址不应选择在靠近城市中心线的地区,因为这里被城市住宅所包围和挤压,而应该由旧城区转移到新港口和新城区,从而建成免受干扰区域的结构并分布开来。

一个好的港址应该不仅有利于港口发展现状,而且同样关注港口未来的发展,例如,关注 30 年后可能的发展状态。

新的港址应与原港区相协调,并满足新的要求。新港址应有利于发挥新旧港口的综合功能,使旧港在更大、更新的基础上仍能发挥作用。

寻找建设新港口的合适地点同时扩展现有的港口需要满足以下的需求:

(1) 泊位处有安全水深及适合航道。

(2) 足够的陆域面积。

(3) 便捷的公路、铁路或水运航线。

第十八课 码头的功能分类

码头作为水运的终端,其分类方法有很多种,这里我们只介绍根据功能进行的分类。

根据货物类型及其包装方式分类

杂货码头。杂货码头采用传统起重机,操纵各种和起重机匹配的包装方式的货物。包装方式可以是捆装、袋装、托盘等等。

多用途码头。这种码头集合了多种功能于一身,集装箱以及传统的普通货物、其他包装货物甚至或者重货都可以在这里被处理。

集装箱码头。在这个码头区域,用特种的装卸、输运和打包设备对集装箱进行操作。

滚装码头。在这种码头货物由滚装系统调运,这种系统采用水平移动的载货卡车、叉车、拖拉机等装卸货物。

专门码头。只有某一种货物可以在这种码头装卸,比如煤码头和油码头等。

根据贸易类型分类

主要负责国外进出口贸易的码头叫做外贸码头,主要负责国内贸易的码头叫做内贸码头。当货物流通只是单向的时候,这种码头通常被称作为国际(或国内)的单一出口或单一进口码头。

根据所有权分类

只为运输一个或者几个公司的原材料或者终端产品的码头叫做专用码头。这种码头通常由使用它们的工厂和矿业投资。由交通部投资给腹地贸易货主提供服务的是公共港口。如果许多种类的货物能够在这处理,我们通常称这种港口为通用港口。

根据服务对象分类

处理货物的码头叫货物码头,服务乘客的码头叫客运码头。

第十九课　防波堤布置原则

近年来,港口结构中超过 20 米的大水深防波堤不再少见。由于防波堤建造成本相对较高,它对港址的选择和港口的布置影响显著。因此,在一些港口,防波堤布置的合理与否对港口的规划布局至关重要。许多因素影响防波堤的布置,例如自然因素,像风、波浪、水流、泥沙、地形和地质情况、使用要求、结构物、投资等。本节将讨论防波堤的布置原则。

防波堤布置原则

防波堤布置应与泊位线相适应,并满足港池内水流平稳的要求。

(1) 长波对船舶的操作和停泊是危险的。周期超过 30 秒或者 1 分钟的波浪,即使波高很小也能引起停泊船只的巨大运动,有时甚至导致锚绳断裂。因此,防波堤应该认真设计以避免港池内长波引起的水体共振,并且阻止波浪穿过防波堤传入港内。

(2) 被防波堤保护的水域应该足够大并且有充足的水深以供船舶移动、停泊和操作。

(3) 保险金支付极限的发展和港口可容纳的极限尺寸船只数目都应该被考虑在港口的未来发展中。

(4) 防波堤保护的水域面积应得到良好的预判。并不是防波堤保护的面积越大越好。切记如果一个港池太大,将会在港池内部产生波浪,这将使船舶停靠变得困难。

在淤泥质海岸地区的港口,更容易使平静水面下的悬疑质泥沙进入港内并产生沉积。因此,一个港口水域越大、纳潮能力越强,港内沉积量就越大。从这一点来看,应尽量减少布置无用水域,从而减少潮流和泥沙进入港口。

(5) 应建立在可用的有利地区,如淹没礁、浅滩、沙坝和浅水区,从而尽可能地节省投资。

第二十课　护　舷

概述

海岸护舷给停靠的船舶和结构物之间提供了必要的界面,因此护舷的主要功能是将停泊船只撞击荷载转变为反作用,使得船只和结构物都可以安全承受。合理设计的护舷系统必须能够平缓地停住运动的或停靠的船只而不损害到船只、结构物或者护舷。当船只停泊并且安全系泊时,护舷系统应该能有足够的强度保护船只和停靠结构物承受住由风、浪、水流、潮差、卸装荷载而产生的外力和位移。护舷的设计还需要考虑船舶和停靠结构物受到的一旦由于能量吸收容量不足导致的事故造成的重要后果。

在以往乃至如今设计泊位和护舷建筑物的过程中,先规划停靠结构物本身,后期才根据泊位和船的需求考虑护舷的类型,这种设计方法导致停靠结构和护舷频繁受损以及稍轻微些的船只受损。

正确的设计步骤应该是对护舷和停靠结构一同规划和设计,选择护舷要依据停泊船只的尺寸和最大冲击能量。护舷标准确定后,停靠结构的上层部分的设计才可以最终确定。因此在选择护舷系统时考虑以下因素:

(1) 护舷系统有足够的能量吸收能力。
(2) 来自护舷系统的反作用力不超过停靠系统的承载力。
(3) 来自护舷系统的外部压力不超过船体的压力承受值。
(4) 同时考虑停靠结构和护舷系统的建造和维护的资金成本。

将会产生以下结果:

(1) 正确的结构方案;
(2) 更少的建设费用;
(3) 更少的年度维护费。

护舷要求

单一或简单的护舷解决方案是不存在的。每种类型的停靠结构都有不同的要求。影响护舷的选择因素有:船舶尺寸、导航方式、位置、潮差、水深等。停靠在开敞区结构物处的船对护舷系统的要求显然比停泊在有保护的结构物处的船要更多一些。

就停靠结构对船舶撞击的"敏感度"而言,一般来说,直立式靠泊结构对水平撞击的抵抗能力较强,而透空式结构抵抗能力较差而且较为敏感。这意味着靠泊结构对停泊冲击的敏感度随其自身的"结构细长度"而增长,并且细长度越大护舷的重要性越强。例如,混凝土块的锚泊结构就不像透空式高桩码头那么脆弱。

  在选择护舷系统时,应该牢记靠泊结构的目的。有特殊功能的结构物通常要提供适应某些类型的船只的护舷,例如,油轮泊位。但是从另一方面看,如果一个泊位需要容纳多种尺寸和类型的船只,如多用途靠泊结构,则护舷系统的选择就困难得多,需要详细的考虑和可能的特殊设计处理。如果泊位处于开敞区域,操纵条件艰难并遇有极端的潮差,选择正确的护舷问题将变得更为复杂。

第二十一课 人工岛

人工岛是人工建造而非自然形成的岛屿。人工岛的大小不一,由扩大现存的小岛、建筑物或暗礁,或合并数个自然小岛建造而成;有时是独立填海而成的小岛,用来支撑建筑物或构造体的单一柱状物,从而支撑其整体。

早期的人工岛是浮动结构,建于静水,或以木制、巨石等在浅水中建造。现在的人工岛大多填海而成,然而,一些是通过运河的建造分割出来的,或者,因为流域泛滥,小丘顶部被水分隔,形成人工岛。此外,一些甚至会以石油平台的方式建造,但是人们对其是否应该称为人工岛存在分歧。

现代人工岛用途广泛。以往,人工岛一部分用于仪式用途,另一部分用于隔离一些人。如今,人工岛可以缓解城市拥挤,兴建机场和促进旅游业。此外,建造人工岛也可以减轻海岸侵蚀或进行可再生能源发电。然而,反对者认为人工岛造价高,对生态环境会造成影响。

近十年来,中国的人工岛建造技术发展迅速。仅在中国的第二大油田胜利油田,就有超过20个人工岛建造完成。

人工岛建造与使用相关要求包括:

1. 软基处理

一般来说,用于建造人工岛的海底天然软土地基需要进行处理和加固。软基处理的方法有许多种,包括开挖换填法、排水固结法、水下挤密砂桩法以及深层振密技术等。建议根据技术和经济因素对不同方法进行比较。

2. 护面和护坦

由于滩浅海恶劣的自然环境条件,人工岛总是受到风、浪、水流和冰等外力的作用。重要的是,为了确保人工岛的稳定性和安全性,保持岛内的回填材料不被海水冲走,需要铺设护面和护坦来保护人工岛的边坡。

3. 环境负荷选择

风、浪、冰等主要环境荷载必须要精确计算,因为它们是影响项目成本的因素。尤其是海冰和地震载荷的计算必须有足够的数据资料,因为这两类载荷是大多数情况下的控制载荷。

4. 监测和检查

在施工与使用期间,必须监测和检查人工岛的稳定性及强度,预测事故发生的可能性并降低风险。一些监测设备需要在施工期间埋设在人工岛内。监测的项目通常包括人工岛基础的沉降量、各组成部分的位移、泥沙冲淤以及结构和材料的剩余强度。

5. 安全和救生

海上救生无疑是非常重要的。每个人工岛必须提供有效的安全和救生设备，如报警装置、救生艇、消防设施等。人工岛在投入使用之前必须制定应急响应方案。

6. 环境保护

目前，海洋环境保护在世界范围内受到了越来越多的重视。对于一些可能产生的污染事故，在人工岛屿设计、建造和使用过程中应制定相关的预防和处理办法。此外，在项目开始之前，应对一些项目应进行评估，包括人工岛建设期间的环境变化、人工岛使用期间对环境的影响以及当岛屿被废弃时的环境危害。

7. 沉箱重复使用

人工岛的组成部分，例如沉箱和大的石头，应该重复使用以减少成本。这也是世界人工岛建设的发展趋势。因此，在沉箱的制造、运输、安装、拆卸和重建过程中应该这一因素，使得整个过程简单、方便和容易操作。

一般来说，人工岛建设的风险较高，需要较高的投资，因此必须满足以下要求：

遵守国家和国际的海洋安全和环境保护的法律和法规。

设计方案应采用先进技术、降低成本、保护环境、确保安全，不仅满足钻井和采油的需要，还要在人工岛退役后可拆卸或移动。

人工岛设计应当遵循一些原则，如结合当地情况调整方案，利用附近的建筑材料和便利措施，缩短海上工作时间等。

第二十二课　浮式生产储油轮

近年来,海上油田开发已经转向更深和更偏远的海域发展,现在这些油田位于超过 5 000 英尺的水深,而这曾被认为不具备开发的经济可行性。此外,新的大型油田,即所谓的大象们,发现率的快速减少,使得开发更小型油田成为必要。FPSO 系统这个概念的提出,降低了油田的最小经济尺寸,并使这些在较深水域的小型或偏远油田的开发成为可能。

正如其缩写所示,FPSO 系统具有(浮动)生产、存储和输运的功能。FPSO 系统经由柔性立管通过安装在转塔上的旋转接头来接收来自海底油储层的流体,然后流体通过工艺设备被分离为油、气和水,并且通常被封装到固定在船体甲板上的模块中(生产功能)。分离的油被存储在船体的液舱中(存储功能),并通过浮动软管装置定期地卸载到穿梭油轮上(卸载功能)。FPSO 系统既在甲板上配备生产设施,又在船体中设有大型液舱。

除了这些功能,FPSO 系统还具有其他功能组件,以确保设施在海上的作业安全。这些组件包括:系泊系统和转塔,用于保持系统在位状态;立管系统和旋转接头,用于接收流体;以及安全和公用设施,用于支持在海上连续作业。

FPSO 系统的几个特性为边际油田的开发带来了优势,列举如下:

水深适应性

浮动结构内在的本质是它们对宽范围水深的适应性。FPSO 系统的概念在 1974 年提出,当时水深 43 米,而今天的 FPSO 系统已安装于 1 400 米的水深。在超深水(1 500~3 000 m)中系泊 FPSO 系统的成本增加小于常规固定式结构或张力腿平台(TLP)。

可预制性

FPSO 系统及所含的工艺装备的建造整合都在造船厂进行,并在出坞之前完成。因为设施的制造与船舶的建造或改造可以各自独立地平行进行,这种方法实现了施工耗时的最小化。如果进行适当的预先调试,也可实现海上现场安装的调试阶段耗时最小化。因此,项目周期时间(从项目开工到初次采油的时间)要短得多,并且与固定结构和一些必须在岸边或离岸配合的张力腿平台(TLP)相比,不遵守时间表的风险更小。

独立性

由于 FPSO 系统在货舱中具有内置的存储能力,不必为连接现有基础设施建造长而昂贵的管道。因此,附近没有管道网络的远海油田可以采用 FPSO 系统进行开发,这样既实现了最低资本支出(CAPEX)又缩短了项目周期时间。

可移植性

一旦油储层耗尽，FPSO 系统可以很容易地以较低的成本被重新定位到另一个油田。这只需要断开立管和系泊系统。经过小修改和/或干船坞检修后，FPSO 系统可以通过连接于新建的系泊系统安装在下一个油田。这个特性给经营者带来了较大的财务优势，因为船舶及其设施的资本成本可以分配给几个项目，这极大地提高了边际油田的经济性。

与其他设施的适配性

FPSO 或浮式存储和卸载(FSO)系统可以与或者不与诸如固定井口平台、海底采油树、张力腿平台(TLP)、浮式生产系统(FPS)等其他设施组合使用。因此，FPSO 系统适用于各种油田开发选项。

原油市场拓展性

使用 FPSO 系统具有能够将原油销售到不同市场的显著优势，从而在当前市场状况下能够实现可能最佳的单桶原油价格。使用管道作为输送机制经常限定产品必须在哪里出售，且通常以更低的单桶原油价格出售。

分离存储

FPSO 系统中的液舱允许同一船舶上分离存储来自不同油井的不同原油，并且因此可避免由于不同质量原油混合引起的问题和价格落差。这一点在处理第三方生产情形下尤其重要。

第二十三课　重力式结构

根据结构设计的不同,重力式结构可以分为以下三种:

(1) 方块码头;

(2) 沉箱码头;

(3) 格型钢板桩码头。

重力式码头结构通常适用于地基良好且沉降风险小的区域。

方块码头

方块码头是最早的码头结构型式,其墙身是按一定方式砌筑而成的。这类码头修建在优良地基上,由坚硬的天然石材或混凝土块组成,经久耐用,维修量小。由于天然石块的开采成本较高,所以现阶段只有使用混凝土块体才是经济可行的。

由于许多新型的船舶具有强大的船首推进器,特别是对于老码头,船舶纵摇运动对墙前结构的破坏已成为一个严重的工程问题。

由于大量的施工作业需要潜水员在水下完成,所以方块码头的施工成本非常高。因此,现阶段这种类型的结构只在特殊的当地条件下才被采用,例如,在坚实的地基上修建的长岸线码头,非技术工人劳动力成本很低,在施工前浇铸足够数量的混凝土块。因此,技术工人的空闲时间将被最小化。为了尽可能减少水下作业量,块体的尺寸应尽可能相同,并且在浇筑块体之后,每一层应首先在岸上布置和标记,以便于其最终放置在水中。

为了保证单个块体的稳定性,块体尺寸应尽量满足起重设备的最大处理能力。

沉箱码头

在沉箱码头中,码头前沿面按照新泊位布置方案,由并排放置预制混凝土沉箱构成。根据现场条件和可用的施工设备的不同,沉箱的形状和设计有很多种。矩形沉箱是最常见的。

沉箱通常在岸上预制,制好后溜放下水,用拖轮拖运到现场所,定好位置,用灌水加载的方法将沉箱子沉放在整平好的抛石基床上。因此,水下工作量小。如果可以利用当地的滑道或干船坞预制下水,那么施工既非常经济又方便。出于经济方面的考虑,沉箱适合大批量生产,这样可以合理地多次使用模板单元。

经验表明,为了便于沉箱的施工、下水、拖运、安放等,从经济的角度出发沉箱长、宽、高通常不应大于 30 m、25 m 和 20 m,但在干船坞中可以预制长度超过 100 m 的混凝土块体。沉箱的设计应满足施工期和使用期的要求。

沉箱通常安放在整平的抛石基床上。非常重要的是,在放置沉箱之前,大部分的沉降量要达到最小值，特别是不均匀沉降量。如果该场地受到波浪和水流的作用，基础和沉箱的设计应使得沉箱下水、拖运和安放时间尽可能缩短。在沉箱安放结束后，向内部填充适当的材料，再盖上钢筋混凝土盖板，这与方块码头施工类似。

与方块码头相比，沉箱码头中的趾板能够有效地减小外缘处的应力。增加沉箱的宽度，或者仅在两隔舱或三隔舱沉箱中的后方隔舱进行填充也可以减小应力。沉箱的设计还应满足生产、下水、拖运、安放和填充期间的荷载和应力要求。

如果沉箱用于阻挡后方回填流失或阻止波浪及水流通过缝隙进入后方，则沉箱之间的所有接头都必须密封。沉箱接头处应根据安放公差和不均匀沉降量设计，受掩护水域的安放公差应为 150 mm。

格形钢板桩码头

近年来，格形钢板桩码头已成为最常见的重力式码头之一。主要原因是方块码头和沉箱码头的劳动力与材料价格比不断提高。板桩码头的几何构造有许多种。

圆形与拱形框格相连平面形状是最常见的构造，每一个圆形框格筒可以单独回填而保持自身稳定。

大直径的格形钢板桩码头是北极水域中最常用的码头结构之一，因为这种类型的码头结构可承受很大的水平力。

格形钢板桩码头提供的优点是：它是无需增加外部锚固结构的稳定的重力式码头。框筒内填充材料的性质必须要严格控制。经验表明，钢板桩在应力作用下互锁，导致其渗透率低，因此要研究是否要在钢板桩上增加排水系统。

第二十四课 港 池

港池是为船舶安全作业提供的受保护水域。港口可分为天然港、半天然港或人工港。港口有不同的用途,如商港、避风港、军港、油港等。

在口门内,港口水域应按功能划分不同的区域,如系泊水域和回转水域。如果港口接纳船舶的类型很多,从经济角度出发,应至少分为两个区域,分别接纳大型和小型船舶,小型船舶应位于港内水深较浅区域。危险品(如石油和天然气)泊位应与其他泊位保持一定的安全距离或净间距。这类作业通常应位于港池外部独立水域和下风向水域。

口门

口门应尽可能布置在港口的下风向。如果它必须位于港口的上风向,则应该充分布置防波堤,以便船舶在通过受限制的口门时,在波浪打到侧舷上之前能够自由转弯。

防波堤的布置能够减少波浪对港口的内部的影响。因此,为了减小港内的波浪高度和水流速度,口门宽度不应超过安全航行所需的必要宽度。

在设计水深处口门宽度的计算取决于港内允许波高以及由船型尺度、交通密度、水深和涨潮落潮流速决定的航行要求。

制动距离

船舶的制动距离取决于船速、船舶位移、形状以及额定功率等因素。假定制动距离足够大,能够使船舶完全制动。下列数据可供粗略参考:对于压载船舶,制动距离为船长的3~5倍。对于满载船舶,制动距离为船长的7~8倍。

回转水域

回转水域通常位于港池的中心区域,其大小取决于使用该区域的船舶的操控性和船长以及执行转弯操纵的时间。该区域应避免波浪和强风的作用。应该记住的压载船舶应减少转向操作。

以下回转水域的最小直径通常被采纳。船舶在不使用船舶推进器和/或拖轮辅助而转向的最小直径约为船长的4倍。使用拖轮协助,则转弯直径取船长的2倍。在良好的天气和操控条件下,回转直径可降低至船长的3倍,个别情况可低至1.6倍。使用主螺旋桨、舵和船舶推进器,转弯直径取船长的1.5倍。水面平静,船舶使用拖轮,并借助码头和靠船墩协助调头时,回转直径最小值可以取船长的1.2倍。

第二十五课 港珠澳大桥

香港—珠海—澳门大桥横跨珠江口伶仃洋，连接香港特别行政区、广东省珠海市和澳门特别行政区。从珠江三角洲东岸的香港口岸到西岸的珠海/澳门口岸全长约42公里。项目的独特之处主要包括：

（1）港珠澳大桥将会是世界上最长的以桥隧组合方式三线双程行车的跨海通道，由北大屿山海岸至珠江西岸全长约35.6公里。

（2）港珠澳大桥需满足120年的设计使用寿命，主桥部分设计和施工的规范除符合内地适用法律及可行性研究报告有关规定，也会适当吸纳香港及澳门合适的相关规范。

（3）港珠澳大桥的建设环境复杂，需要考虑频繁的台风、纵横交错的航道、航道空限高及环保方面的要求等。

（4）为减少大桥建设对河势、航道、水利等的不利影响，在进行大桥建设方案比选时严格控制阻水比。

采用大跨度的跨海高架桥梁

西部跨海高架桥是由大跨度桥梁所组成，主跨度为75至180米。鉴于走线位置同时位于机场西面船只航道之上，故海上桥梁在跨越船只航道时，桥身的水平位置会相应提升以提供41米的净空高度供船只通过。这条双程三线分隔公路将配备有一个车辆掉头设施，供紧急情况或管理运作时使用。

沿机场水道采取特别措施以减少对自然环境的影响

香港接线跨海高架桥梁段的东面会进入位处于香港国际机场及北大屿山之间的机场水道。为减少对现有自然环境的干扰，这段香港接线采取了若干措施，包括采用跨度较大的高架桥梁跨越大屿山散石湾和沙螺湾之间的陆岬而无须触及大屿山的土地，减少在沙螺湾一带桥墩的数目以减轻对景观的影响，将高架桥的桩帽埋藏于海床之下，以减少对机场水道水流的影响，并脱离受机场净空限制的地方，尽快把走线靠近机场岛，远离大屿山海岸。

优化地面道路

为了创造优美的环境，位处机场岛东部海岸线，1.6公里长的地面道路沿线特提供广泛的环境美化工程。

提供完善的交通网络

作与港珠澳大桥主桥、香港口岸、屯门至赤鱲角连接路所组成的整体项目，香港接线将密切与其他工程项目交接，有效地把港珠澳大桥连接至毗邻的香港国际机场以及屯门和北大屿山地区,从而形成一个策略性的交通网络,令港珠澳大桥能发挥最大的效益,务求在项目实施过程和将来运作取得整体效益和效率。

香港口岸的非浚挖式填海方案

传统海堤是建造在稳固的基层上,须把海堤下的淤泥浚挖,并回填砂料。这个过程要浚挖及倾倒大量淤泥。为尽量减低浚挖和倾倒淤泥对环境的影响,路政署为位于香港国际机场东北海面、面积约150公顷的人工岛(包括约20公顷屯门至赤鱲角连接路南面填海)开发一套香港首次采用的非浚挖式填海方法。

口岸人工岛部分海堤建造方法是把大直径的钢圆筒压下海床,穿越淤泥层,其后以惰性建筑废料或砂料回填钢圆筒内。通过上述非浚挖式填海方法,可大幅减少浚挖和倾倒淤泥量达2 200万立方米,也会减少使用约一半回填物料。此外,填海工程在施工期间对水质的影响会较少,而海上工程交通量也会大幅减少。这将有助于维护海洋生态,特别是中华白海豚的栖息地。

与传统海堤填海方法比较,非浚挖式填海方法有很多好处,其中包括:

(1) 减少约97%淤泥浚挖及倾倒量;
(2) 减少约一半回填物料用量;
(3) 减少约70%的沉积物悬浮量;
(4) 减少约一半建筑期间海上交通量。

采用隧道钻挖机建造海底隧道

穿越屯门及香港口岸之间的龙鼓水道而兴建的海底隧道将以两台直径约14米的隧道钻挖机建造。与传统的沉管方法相比,以隧道钻挖机建造海底隧道能避免挖掘和弃置为数约1 100万立方米的淤泥。

采用隧道钻挖机建造方法亦可避免对现时为香港国际机场供电的海底电缆进行改道,减低在建造期间对繁忙的龙鼓水道的海上交通的影响,以及减低工程施工期间对工地及附近的海洋生态的影响,例如对中华白海豚的影响。大直径的钻挖海底隧道在香港是史无前例的,对香港工程界而言更是一项重大挑战。

第二十六课 Spar

　　Spar 平台是一种典型的适用于超深水域的浮动采油平台,并以在航运中用作浮标的垂直锚泊的原木命名。Spar 生产平台是作为传统平台的一种替代形式被开发的出来了。Spar 平台的深吃水设计使他们受风、浪、流的影响较小,并同时适用于干式采油树和海底生产。

　　Spar 平台由支撑甲板的大直径单立式圆柱组成。圆柱通过在底部的一个腔室填充比水更致密的材料来配重,以降低平台的重心并提供稳定性。此外,Spar 主体环向布设着螺旋列板用以缓解涡激运动的影响。Spar 通过由链—线—链或链—聚酯—链构造组成的扩展式系泊系统长期锚定在海床上。

　　有三种主要类型的 Spar:经典式 Spar,桁架式 Spar 和集束式 Spar。经典式 Spar 由三个部分组成。上部围绕一个包含不同类型立管的淹没的中心井划分,这部分提供了 Spar 的浮力。中间部分也被淹没,但是从经济性上配置可以用于储油。底部被划分用以在运输期间提供浮力及容纳任何现场安装的固定压载物。

　　桁架式 Spar 具有比经典式 Spar 更短的圆柱形"硬舱",并且具有连接到硬舱底部的桁架结构。该桁架结构由四个大的正交带有 X 形支架的"腿"构件和中间深度处的用以提供阻尼的垂荡板组成。在桁架结构的底部,有一个较小的龙骨或一个容纳重压载材料软舱。软舱通常是矩形的,但也曾有圆形的,以适应特定的构造问题。大多数 Spar 是这种类型。

　　第三种类型的 Spar,即集束式 Spar,有一个大的由不同长度的较小圆柱包围的中心圆柱。在较长圆柱的底部是容纳重压载材料的软舱,类似于桁架式 Spar。集束式 Spar 的设计仅曾用于一个平台:Red Hawk Spar,它在 2014 年安全和环境执法局的"Rigs-to-Reefs"计划退役。在其退役时,它是已退役平台中最深的浮动平台。

　　深水中的油气勘探已经促进了适合此类深度的海洋结构的需求。Spar 平台是这样一种用于深海海洋沉积物的钻井、生产、加工和储存的顺应式的浮式结构物。下面给出了对 Spar 平台技术发展的回顾,包括动力响应、系泊系统、疲劳和耦合分析的研究以及垂荡板和列板配置的设计。

　　与张力腿平台(TLP)相比,Spar 用于中小型钻台的构建也许更经济,并且比张力腿平台(TLP)具有更大的固有稳定性,因为其在底部具有大的配重,且不依赖系泊就可保持竖直。它还具有在油田上方水平移动的能力,这是因为其水线面积小并通过使用链条起重器连接系泊缆线。

　　在陆上装配之后,船体被运输到目的地,然后起重机驳船使主体顶端朝上。当主体松动地保持在适当位置时,泵船填充船体的下压载舱并且淹没中心井使船体自身顶端朝上。接下来，井架驳船升起作为临时工作甲板，用于基本设施挂接、系泊绳附接和立管安装。

船体通过拖船和辅助定位系统被定位于目标位置。然后，系泊系统被连接到主体。在系泊系统连接之后，缆线被施加预张力。然后船体被压载，以准备水线以上部分安装和临时工作甲板的移除。

水线以上部分通过物料驳船运输到海上，并通过井架驳船提升到位。

要安装的最后一批设备是浮力舱和相关的阀门。浮力舱被简单地从材料驳船上卸下并放入中心井区域内的槽中。接下来，阀门被接到浮力舱上。

第二十七课　结构选择

1. 概述

建造任何重要结构之前,宜首先比较各种不同的型式,然后根据基建资金和维修费用或施工难易程度做出合适的选择。在不同情况下,使用同一标准设计可能并不经济适用。本规范虽然给出了典型的结构设计,但并不排除综合两个或多个结构型式的代案。

2. 结构型式

海工建筑物可以是实体的,也可以是透空桩基的。透空桩基结构可以是刚性的,也可以是柔性的。

实体结构包括所有垂直靠墙面的实体板墙和重力式墙。这种结构最常使用于必须挡住填筑材料的顺岸泊位,但这种结构也常用于突堤码头、栈桥和系靠船墩。

透空结构具有以桩为支撑的悬空面板,可以是只有直桩而没有外部水平约束力的柔性结构,也可以是有斜桩或支撑于岸的,更为坚固的刚性结构。柔性的程度取决于总的轮廓、框架、构件及其支撑物的相对刚度。用柔性形式的结构支撑起重机或散货装卸设备,可能是不合适的,尤其在地震地区。

因在施工中或施工后产生主动土压力和被动土抗力,后方挡土的许多种码头结构都略有位移。位移可能是水平位移,也可能是伴有向前旋转的水平位移。这些位移并非自然沉降,而导致位移的决定性因素是结构类型和地基情况。对于以码头结构为一支点或者以主动楔体内的挡土为一支点跨到远离该支点的另一地基支点的固定上部结构,应当考虑这些移动对于固定上部结构的影响。在为新建码头选择结构型式时,宜考虑邻近已有结构的影响。在泊位处和邻近地点,透空桩基结构使目前海洋规律发生的变化很可能要小于实体结构引起的变化,这是因为透空桩基结构对潮流和波浪的阻力相对较小。在易发生淤积的地方,实体结构可使海水流速增快,从而减少岩结构的淤积量,但很可能对其他地方带来不利影响。实体结构造成的反射波浪可对泊位上的船舶有过强的扰动作用,但可通过正面开洞或部分敞开的方式减小扰动。当透空结构用于顺岸泊位时,泊位后方通常有一护岸,用来挡住泊位后方的填土,护岸还可用来吸收波浪能量而减少反射。

可利用柔性结构的弹性变位吸收靠泊船舶的部分或全部能量。

无论选择哪种结构型式,设计时宜留有充分余地,使设计结构能够适应施工过程中可能遇到的现场情况变化。

3. 海底情况

地质资料的收集和水深测量工作宜齐头并进,为不同结构型式寻找适合的基础标高,确定应不应疏浚、是否经济实惠。

4. 当地建筑材料

无论进行何种地质勘察,都宜研究当地可能有的天然建筑材料。在短运程内有石料或一般回填料,可对结构的选择有很大的影响。

5. 施工方法

施工方法、施工顺序以及可提供的主要施工机具可决定结构型式的最终选择。为早日竣工,可尽量使用预制构件,但构件的尺寸和重量必须在可提供机具的吊运能力范围之内。当施工项目属于大项目的一部分时,着眼整个大项目来调遣专用设备和建立大型预制场,可节省费用。如果全年或季节性地使用浮动机具时,天气条件都太坏,可能有必要在岸上建一临时堤进行施工,也可从岸线开始向前逐步施工或在顶升趸船上施工。

6. 施工难度

设计时宜考虑到,施工通常是在水上的临时工作平台上,湍急的浪潮会增加准确施工的难度。在水上施工往往不能达到路上建筑工程中正常的误差。特别宜记住的是,在水上打的桩难以起到全部长度的支撑作用,因为虽然可在海底准确定位,但桩头可偏离正确的位置。因此,在设计桩上的上部构件时,宜使其能适应桩基的允许偏差。在陆上实施开挖,可仔细控制;而在水下,则必须由挖泥船,有时也由潜水员实施。挖泥船会留下波状或台阶状的痕迹,在其表面可淤积一层细粒材料。宜记住,通常实际误差可大于超挖误差(砂、粉土和软黏土中为 0.3 m),所有超挖的凹槽中可能充满软泥。因此,宜考虑经常发生开挖不平整、基层下面形成一层潜在破坏面的可能。在回填前,可在海底放置一层砾石或块石,阻止填料下破坏面的形成。对于可能淤积软土的临时斜坡,其斜面宜与土中潜在破坏面的斜面方向相反。

当预制构件放置在海底的砾石基床上时,最后的整平和机床准备工作必须由潜水员来完成,但由于可见度往往很差,因此宜尽可能使潜水员的工作简单易行。

施工中宜做好充分的保护工作,避免遭到漂浮船舶、波浪和潮流的破坏。

第二十八课　荷　载

1. 概述

关于荷载和土压力宜参考英国标准 BS 6349(1984 年版)第一分册第五章。关于海工建筑物承受的静水压力宜参考英国标准 BS 6349(1984 年版)第一分册第六章。关于护舷和系泊设施宜参考英国标准 BS 6349(1984 年版)第四分册。

初步设计时,可按 2 中所给总标题将荷载分组,但在不寻常或极其关键的情况下,则应分别考虑组内各种荷载。

2. 荷载种类

(1) 恒载

恒载是建筑物结构构件的有效重量。对某些设计分析来说,最好分别考虑构件在大气中的重量和由于静水压力产生的上浮力。这在考虑承压水影响时,尤为重要。

(2) 附加恒载

附加恒载是建筑物上形成荷载的全部材料的重量,而非结构构件的重量。卸载平台上的填料、铺面、装卸货物的固定设备和码头上装置都是典型的附加恒载。在固定轨道上缓慢行走的大型起重机,如集装箱起重机的自重,也属于这一类。

由于移去附加恒载可能会降低整体稳定性或削弱作用在结构另一部分上的卸荷效果,因此在任何分析中都宜考虑移去附加恒载造成的影响。

(3) 可变荷载

在英国标准 BS 6349(1984 年版)第一分册第 47.2 条中,可变荷载被分为如下几类:

①周期荷载;

②冲击荷载;

③随机荷载;

④静荷载和永久周期荷载。

前三类是动力荷载,计算结构反应时,有必要予以分别考虑。

周期荷载和随机荷载主要是环境荷载,而周期荷载也有可能是车流或机械振动引起的。设计时,宜选择可变静荷载和永久周期荷载对结构破坏性最严重的位置和组合。

(4) 土和剩余水荷载

土和剩余水荷载是影响挡土结构稳定性的主要荷载。扰动力受挡土上的超载和可变荷载的影响。

(5) 环境荷载

由于环境荷载具有长期性质,因此环境荷载的影响,比如雪、冰、温度、水流、潮汐和定期平均风的影响,不被认为是动荷载。

周期荷载是由规则的波列和稳定流中的涡流引起的。波浪的冲击力被认为是冲击荷载,而随机荷载包括波浪荷载、由波浪引起的荷载、地震荷载和阵风荷载。

3. 关于整体稳定性的荷载组合

(1) 概述

3.2 至 3.4 中给出的荷载情况并不是唯一的,也宜分析可能发生的其他任何一种临界情况。虽然某些荷载组合是相互独立的,但也要评估两个或多个大荷载同时施加于结构上的可能性。根据破坏结果来看,大多数情况下,以同时施加所有可能的极端荷载来设计是不经济的。而当两个大荷载同时发生的可能性非常低时,可降低安全系数,进行结构分析。

(2) 正常荷载情况

正常荷载是在正常作业情况下,预计可能在结构设计的使用期内,合理发生的任何荷载组合,应包括可预见的结构修改、土方工程、铺面、堆存模式、装卸设备或挖浚深度。

对于第 3.1 条,宜在组合中考虑第 2 条所述的每一类荷载的最大正常值。正常荷载情况如下:

①在规定误差内的海底超挖;

②在计划不超过一年的定期检查期内发生的蓄水港池泄降引起的静水头的增加;

③大潮平均高潮位和大潮平均低潮位的潮位差;

④通常重现期为一年的环境荷载或对港口作业有限制的环境荷载,但不包括地震和海啸;

⑤英国标准 BS 6349 第四分册中所述的靠泊作业;

⑥根据英国标准 BS 8002 从平均土指标导出的荷载;

⑦堆存超过一层箱高,采用分类系数时集装箱的荷载。

(3) 极端荷载情况

极端荷载是指在结构设计使用期内预计可能发生的任何荷载组合,以及实际上可能施加的最严重的可靠荷载,但不包括意外荷载,如失控靠船引起的荷载。宜评估随时发生多于一种极端荷载的可能性。宜认真考虑这种荷载对其他荷载产生的次生影响,比如地震或洪水对土质的影响。

然而,也宜考虑因长期使用而可能发生的变化,比如排水系统有可能在最可靠荷载作用期内发生恶化。极端荷载情况举例如下:

①海底受到冲刷的作用而加深；
②临时的检查或闸门的意外损坏使蓄水港池泄降，进而导致静水头的增加；
③超出正常范围的极端水位；
④重现期与结构物使用期相同的环境荷载；
⑤英国标准 BS 6349 第四分册中所述的异常靠船作业；
⑥土壤指标上四分点或下四分点导出的荷载，取最大值；
⑦在未采用分类系数情况下，集装箱的荷载；
⑧地震和海啸。
（4）施工期临时荷载
宜认真考虑每一阶段预计可发生的荷载。

第二十九课　设　计

1. 设计义务一般要求

承包商应被视为在基准日期前已仔细审查了雇主要求(包括设计标准和计算,如果有)。承包商应负责工程的设计,并在除下列雇主应负责的部分外,对雇主要求(包括设计标准和计算)的正确性负责。

除下述情况外,雇主不应对原包括在合同内的雇主要求中的任何错误、不准确、或遗漏负责,并不应被认为,对任何数据或资料给出了任何准确性或完整性的表示。承包商从雇主或其他方面收到任何数据或资料,不应解除承包商对设计和工程施工承担的职责。

但是,雇主应对雇主要求中的下列部分,以及由(或代表)雇主提供的下列数据和资料的正确性负责:

(1) 在合同中规定的由雇主负责的或不可变的部分、数据和资料;
(2) 对工程或其任何部分的预期目的的说明;
(3) 竣工工程的试验和性能的标准;
(4) 除合同另有说明外,承包商不能核实的部分、数据和资料。

2. 承包商文件

承包商文件应包括雇主要求中规定的技术文件、为满足所有规章要求报批的文件以及第5.6款[竣工文件]和第5.7款[操作和维修手册]中所述的文件。除非雇主要求中另有说明,承包商文件应使用第1.4款[法律和语言]规定的交流语言书写。

承包商应编制所有的承包商文件,还应编制指导承包商人员所需要的任何其他文件。

如果雇主要求中描述了要提交雇主审核的承包商文件,这些文件应依照要求,连同下文叙述的通知一并上报。在本款下列规定中,(1)"审核期"系指雇主审核需要的期限,以及(2)"承包商文件"不包括未规定要提交审核的任何文件。

除非雇主要求中另有说明,每项审核期不应超过21天,从雇主收到一份承包商文件和承包商通知的日期算起。该通知应说明,本承包商文件是已可供按照本款进行审核和使用。通知还应说明本承包商文件符合合同规定的情况或在哪些范围不符合。

雇主在审核期可向承包商发出通知,指出承包商文件(在说明的范围)不符合合同的规定。如果承包商文件确实如此不符合,该文件应由承包商承担费用,按照本款修正、重新上报并审核。

除双方另有协议的范围外,对工程每一部分都应:

(1) 在有关该部分的设计和施工的承包商文件的审核期尚未期满前,不得开工;

(2) 该部分的实施,应按上报审核的承包商文件进行;

(3) 如果承包商希望对已送审的设计或文件进行修改,应立即通知雇主,然后,承包商应按照前述程序将修改后的文件提交雇主。

(根据前一段的)任何协议,或(根据本款或其他条款的)任何审核,都不应解除承包商的任何义务或职责。

3. 承包商的承诺

承包商承诺其设计、承包商文件、实施和竣工的工程符合:

(1) 工程所在国的法律;

(2) 经过变更做出更改或修正的构成合同的各项文件。

4. 技术标准和法规

设计、承包商文件、施工和竣工工程,均应符合工程所在国的技术标准、建筑、施工与环境方面的法律、适用于工程将生产的产品的法律以及雇主要求中提出的适用于工程或适用法律规定的其他标准。

所有这些关于工程和其各分项工程的法规,应是在雇主根据第10条[雇主的接收]的规定接收工程或分项工程时通行的。除非另有说明,合同中提到的各项已公布标准应视为在基准日期适用的版本。

如果在基准日期后,上述版本有修改或有新的标准生效,承包商应通知雇主,并(如适宜)提交遵守新标准的建议书。如果:

(1) 雇主确定需要遵守;

(2) 遵守新标准的建议书构成一项变更时,雇主应按照第13条[变更和调整]的规定着手做出变更。

第三十课　承包商

1. 承包商的一般义务

承包商应按照合同设计、实施和完成工程,并修补工程中的任何缺陷。完成后,工程应能满足合同规定的工程预期目的。

承包商应提供合同规定的生产设备和承包商文件,以及设计、施工、竣工和修补缺陷所需的所有临时性或永久性的承包商人员、货物、消耗品及其他物品和服务。

工程应包括为满足雇主要求或合同隐含要求的任何工作,以及(合同虽未提及但)为工程的稳定、或完成、或安全和有效运行所需的所有工作。

承包商应对所有现场作业、所有施工方法和全部工程的完备性、稳定性和安全性承担责任。

当雇主提出要求时,承包商应提交其建议采用的工程施工安排和方法的细节。事先未通知雇主,对这些安排和方法不得做重要改变。

2. 履约担保

承包商应对严格履约(自费)取得履约担保,保证金额与币种应符合专用条件中的规定。专用条件中没有提出保证金额的,本款应不适用。

承包商应在双方签署合同协议书后28天内,将履约担保交给雇主。履约担保应由雇主批准的国家(或其他司法管辖区)内的实体提供,并采用专用条件所附格式或采用雇主批准的其他格式。

承包商应确保履约担保直到其完成工程的施工、竣工和修补完任何缺陷前持续有效和可执行。如果在履约担保的条款中规定了其期满日期,而承包商在该期满日期28天前尚无权拿到履约证书,承包商应将履约担保的有效期延至工程竣工和修补完任何缺陷时为止。

除出现以下情况雇主根据合同有权获得的金额外,雇主不应根据履约担保提出索赔:

(1)承包商未能按前一段所述延长履约担保的有效期,这时雇主可以索赔履约担保的全部金额;

(2)承包商未能在商定或确定后42天内,将承包商同意的,或根据第2.5款[雇主的索赔]或第20条[索赔、争端和仲裁]的规定确定的承包商应付金额付给雇主;

(3)承包商未能在收到雇主要求纠正违约的通知后42天内进行纠正;或

(4)根据第15.2款[由雇主终止]的规定,雇主有权终止的情况,不管是否已发出终止通知。

雇主应保障并保持承包商免受因雇主根据履约担保提出的超出雇主有权索赔范围的索赔引起的所有损害赔偿费、损失和开支（包括法律费用和开支）的伤害。

雇主应在承包商有权获得履约证书后21天内，将履约担保退还承包商。

3. 承包商代表

承包商应任命承包商代表，并授予他代表承包商根据合同采取行动所需要的全部权力。除非合同中已写明承包商代表的姓名，承包商应在开工日期前，将其拟任命为承包商代表的人员姓名和详细资料提交给雇主，以取得同意。如果未获同意，或随后撤销了同意，或任命的人不能担任承包商代表，承包商应同样地提交另外适合人选的姓名、详细资料，以取得该项任命。

未经雇主事先同意，承包商不应撤销承包商代表的任命，或任命何替代人员。

承包商代表应代表承包商受理根据第3.4款[指示]规定的指示。

承包商代表可向任何胜任的人员付托任何职权、任务和权力，并可随时撤销付托。任何付托或撤销，应在雇主收到承包商代表签发的指明人员姓名、并说明付托或撤销的职权、任务和权力的事先通知后生效。

承包商代表和所有这些人员应能流利地使用第1.4款[法律和语言]规定的交流语言。

4. 分包商

承包商不得将整个工程分包出去。

承包商应对任何分包商、其代理人或雇员的行为或违约，如同承包商自己的行为或违约一样地负责。对专用条件中有规定的，承包商应在不少于28天前向雇主通知以下事项：

(1) 拟雇用的分包商，并附包括其相关经验的详细资料；

(2) 分包商承担工作的拟定开工日期；

(3) 分包商承担现场工作的拟定开工日期。

参 考 文 献

1. P Novak, A I B Moffat, C Nalluri, R Narayanan. Hydraulic Structures (4th edition). Oxon: Taylor & Francis, 2007.

2. 迟道才,周振民. 水利专业英语. 北京:中国水利水电出版社,2006.

3. Hubert Chanson. The Hydraulics of Open Channel Flow. Oxford: Elsevier Butterworth-Heinemann, 2004.

4. Thomas J Pokrefke P E. Inland Navigation Channel Training Works. USA: American Society of Civil Engineers, 2012.

5. 陈一梅,廖鹏. 港口规划与布置(英文版). 南京:东南大学出版社,2009.

6. Carl A Thoresen. Port Design. Norway: Tapir, 1988.

7. 王秉钧,郭正行. 科技英汉汉英翻译技巧. 天津:天津大学出版社,1999.

8. 徐勇,王志刚. 英语科技论文翻译与写作教程. 北京:化学工业出版社出版,2015.

9. 方天中. 汉英土木和港口工程词典. 北京:人民交通出版社,2009.

10. 林鸿慈. 英汉港口航道工程词典(第二版). 北京:人民交通出版社,1997.

11. 国际咨询工程师联合会. 菲迪克合同指南—应用菲迪克(FIDIC)1999年第1版合同条件的详细指南. 中国工程咨询协会,编译. 北京:机械工业出版社,2003.

12. 李华晔,刘汉东,王四巍,于怀昌. 地质与岩土工程专业英语. 郑州:黄河水利出版社,2008.

13. 贾艳敏. 工程英语. 北京:人民交通出版社,2006.

14. 贾艳敏. 土木工程专业英语. 北京:科学出版社,2011.

15. 雷自学. 土木工程专业英语. 北京:知识产权出版社,2010.

16. 霍俊芳,姜丽云. 土木工程专业英语. 北京:北京大学出版社,2010.

17. 熊英. 工程管理专业英语教程. 北京:电子工业出版社,2009.

后 记

  港口航道与海岸工程专业英语不仅是大学英语教学的一个重要组成部分,也是专业课教学的重要内容,是促进学生们完成从英语和专业知识学习过渡到实际应用的有效途径。学习专业英语可以培养学生以英语为工具进行专业知识交流的能力。

  本书主要分为基础知识、港口工程、航道工程、海岸工程、规范与合同5个模块,共30篇课文,所涉及的内容包括:土木工程、水利工程、测量、工程地质、航道运输、航道整治、港口规划布置、人工岛、跨海大桥、工程规范及合同等方面。通过学习这本教材,学生们不仅可以熟悉和掌握港口航道与海岸工程专业常用的及与专业有关的单词和词组,而且可以深化本专业的知识,从而为今后的学习和工作打下良好的基础。

  本书由上海海事大学辛凌,大连海洋大学郑艳娜、崔蕾、刘昌凤,广东海洋大学杨章峰、佟珉霞六位老师共同编写,具体分工如下:辛凌主要编写了第一模块,崔蕾主要编写了第二模块,郑艳娜主要编写了第三模块,刘昌凤主要编写了第四模块,杨章峰和佟珉霞主要编写了第五模块。郑艳娜和杨章峰负责全书的统稿和校对。

  本书的编写得到了大连海洋大学陈昌平教授、桂劲松教授,上海海事大学史旦达教授的大力支持和指导,大连海洋大学研究生刘心媚也参加了书稿的整理工作,在此表示衷心感谢!由于作者的理论水平和实践经验所限,本书难免有疏漏和不足之处,敬请各位读者不吝赐教,批评指正,以便我们予以改进!

郑艳娜
2017 年 1 月